subUrbia

subUrbia

eric bogosian

revised edition

theatre communications group
new york
2009

subUrbia is published by Theatre Communications Group, Inc., 520 8th Avenue, 24th Floor, New York, NY 10018–4156

The first edition of *subUrbia* was published in 1995.

This publication is made possible in part with public funds from the New York State Council on the Arts, a State Agency.

TCG books are exclusively distributed to the book trade by Consortium Book Sales and Distribution.

Library of Congress Cataloging-in-Publication Data

Bogosian, Eric.
subUrbia / Eric Bogosian.—1st rev. ed.
p. cm.
ISBN 978-1-55936-342-6
1. Young adults—Drama. 2. Suburban life—Drama. 3. Generation X—Drama.
I. Title.
PS3552.O46S83 2009
812'.54—dc22   2009013802

Cover illustration by Frank Kozik
Cover design by Jo Bonney
Text design and composition by Lisa Govan

First Revised Edition, November 2009

To André Bishop, a man of faith

The Story of the Garden Gnome

A Preface

When we did *subUrbia* at Lincoln Center in 1994, we got Frank Kozik to design the poster because at the time Frank Kozik was (and as far as I know, pretty much still is) the most intense and imaginative poster artist out there. He designed and illustrated tour posters for Nirvana and Sonic Youth (Sonic Youth ended up composing the score for the film of *subUrbia*) and many others. He brought the right mix of speed and fun.

Frank asked what we needed on the poster. We replied that the poster should probably feature a slice of pizza, maybe a doughnut, a handgun?

When we got Frank's design all those things were there. Pizza, gun, doughnut. But there was something additional, the face of a troll-like man. What was it?

Frank replied that this was a garden gnome. Very suburban. Garden gnomes exist in the thousands all over the American suburbs. Frank felt there should be a face in the poster.

We said, OK. Whatever. Good. Posters and postcards were printed. They looked great. I handed them out to friends. Whereupon someone asked me, indicating the gnome, "What's that?"

I said, "It's a little suburban statue. A garden gnome. People put them in their gardens."

"Oh," she said. "Is there a garden gnome in your play?"

"No. No gnome," I said. But then I understood there *should* be a garden gnome in my play.

When we began rehearsals at Lincoln Center, I adjusted dialogue, wrote bits of text. And one day I showed up with a scene in which Buff (played by Steve Zahn) runs off drunk and returns carrying a freshly stolen garden gnome. The new scene worked. Later, when Rick Linklater made the film of the play, we expanded the garden gnome scene so that the merry troll joined the cast in their ride in the limo! It became a major scene in the film.

I share this story because it's a good illustration of how the different folks who worked on the play (and the film) all threw in. Frank Kozik, Robert Falls, Steve Zahn, then Rick Linklater later on. Layer upon layer, we built this play, from a workshop at the American Repertory Theater in Cambridge, to Juilliard, to Lincoln Center, in Austin making the film, and at Second Stage when Jo Bonney directed. That's what theater is. Everyone throwing in. Showing up to play.

Eric Bogosian
New York
August 2009

Introduction

I grew up in Woburn, Massachusetts, about ten miles northwest of Boston. Like most suburbs, its history is a nasty collision between past, present and future.

A stately Methodist church, a small green with a "minuteman," and a stone library grace the center of the city. So does a small marker memorializing the men who died in the Vietnam War. The local myth is that two hundred years earlier Paul Revere rode through what is now a strip of woods separating the housing developments.

In the late 1800s my hometown was a hotbed of Industrial Revolution–type activity. (Rubber was first vulcanized in Woburn!) Because of the lax environmental laws in the bad old days, the soil in parts of Woburn is among the most toxic in the whole United States.

Our fair town has seen mayors indicted for corruption, has given birth to top football and hockey teams. Nancy Kerrigan is from one town over.

Woburn has grown from being an aging industrial hamlet to a teeming professional community intersected by I-95's high-tech corridor. America's first really big shopping mall was built off the highway. When I was sixteen, I hung out at that mall and shopped for Hush Puppies. When I was twenty and a college dropout I worked at the new Gap store. Now I go there and get nostalgic.

As I was growing up, as the mall and the high-tech factories were built, the local roads and highways got busier and busier. Thirty years ago the mini-mall where I first hung out, "Four Corners," had a barbershop, a pharmacy and a furniture store. Now a 7-Eleven, a Burger King and a car dealership stand in their place. Looking at Four Corners now, it's hard to believe anyone ever had a personal feeling for the place. But I did. It's where I came of age. I fell in love there, got drunk there, got in fights. (One time, Mikey Turner bit a chunk out of me in the parking lot of the Dunkin' Donuts. Had the scar for six years.)

For the people who first moved to Woburn, the suburbs represented escape, fresh air, order and lack of crime. But for those of us who grew up in the suburbs, the suburbs didn't *represent* anything, they *were* something: home. Suburbs were not an escape from reality, they were reality.

Not until I went to school in Chicago, did I realize there was any place *not* like Woburn. My home is a strange home, a home full of contradictions. A community, but not a community, a place, but not a place. And as Joel Garreau points out in his study *Edge City*: a city, but not a city. (One of the chapters is devoted to our local mall and environs.)

This territory is where I come from, where lots of other people come from, too. If you grow up in the suburbs, you are told over and over again that you are living the American Dream. But if you are like me, you're not so sure. If you are like me, you leave the American Dream.

The strangest aspect of growing up where I grew up is thinking you know everything about the world, when in fact you know nothing. This is the story of me and mine, as it continues today, all over America.

Eric Bogosian
New York
April 1995

Acknowledgments

*S*ub*Urbia* started out when my friend, Bob Riley, then at the Institute of Contemporary Art in Boston, suggested I try something larger than solo work. Fred Zollo had been encouraging me for years to write about the town we grew up in, and so with a grant from the Massachusetts Council on the Arts and Humanities, the play began sometime around 1986. Later Bob Brustein was kind enough to let me "workshop" the initial writing on the piece with his students at the American Repertory Theater in Cambridge. That was in 1989. And again, in 1992, Anne Cattaneo arranged a workshop production with students at Juilliard.

Many people have helped shape this play, nudged it toward the magnificent production it received at Lincoln Center Theater in 1994. I would like to thank:

At the Institute of Contemporary Art in Boston: Bob Riley and David Ross.

Acknowledgments

At A.R.T: Bob Brustein; Rob Orchard; Julie Miles; Rebecca Rickman; the cast—Ellen Kohrman, Ross Salinger, Chris Colt, Steve Zahn, Celeste Ciulla, Sean Runnette, Dean Harrison and my assistant, Jeff Zinn.

At Juilliard: Michael Kahn; my invaluable stage manager Pat Sosnow; Clifford Berek; Isaac Ho; George Xenos; Chele Ware; Caroline Seltzer; Lisa Renee; and the cast—Maya Thomas, Chris McKinney, C. J. Wilson, Brian Kelly, Jeff Stafford, Carrie Preston, Lauren Lovett, Dallas Roberts, Nicole Marcks and Danny Mastrogiorgio.

Recipe for a brilliant, mind-altering production: start with script; add Robert Falls; fold in a totally driven, young-genius cast; set blender speed at "whiplash" and wait for the subscribers to walk out. Thank you Bob, Firdous, Tim, Josh, Wendy, Zak, Martha, Reneé, Samia and Steve—you made my dream come true.

Heartfelt thanks to Bernie and André and to our wonderful design team: Derek, Ken, Gabriel and John. To Annie Cattaneo for tea and sympathy. And to our ever-patient and loving production stage manager Christopher Wigle and stage manager Miriam Auerbach. Thanks to Liz Timperman for making sure this text was letter-perfect for performance. And thanks to our sturdy understudies: Nick Rodgers, Jon Patrick Walker, Aasif Mandviwala, Maya Israel and Anney Giobbe.

Lincoln Center Theater is a big place. I'm sure I don't know everyone who made this show go. But special thanks to Daniel Swee, Jean Bacharach, Steve Callahan, Ed Nelson, Julie Crosby, Patrick Herold, Mari Eckroate, Mala Yee, Jeff Hamlin, Merle Debuskey, Susan Chicoine, David Leong, Julia Judge, Beth Emelson, Alison Laslett, Norma Fire, Graeme McDonnell and Bonnie Runk.

One final point on the Lincoln Center production of this text: Zak Orth wrote and played the music that accompanied my lyrics for the songs. And Samia Shoaib created the Urdu text as spoken by her character. Martha Plimpton created her performance from my text. And Tim Guinee and Steve Zahn did all their own stunts.

subUrbia wouldn't exist at all without many, many people adding their creative excellence:

Of course, none of this could have succeeded without an amazing director. Robert Falls had the vision and strength to pull this circus together back in 1994. I can't thank him enough.

Steve Zahn was a cast member in three productions; a clutch of seniors at Juilliard worked out the original beats. In addition, there was the staff of casting people, producers, designers, who all worked on this project along the way. Later when we shot the film, more creative input poured in. Later still, when the play was remounted in 2006, new shades of character arrived in the form of a cast who were in grade school when the first production went up. Jo Bonney directed the play twice: in Washington, D.C., and at Second Stage in New York. She asked for specific rewrites each time. There have been many productions beyond what we've done, but, specifically, productions at the University of Southern California and Brooklyn College contributed cast members who would appear in both the later stage and film versions.

Special thanks to all my good friends who make it work: George Lane, Michael Carlisle, Ron Taft, Philip Rinaldi and Edith Meeks.

Special thanks to Nikole Beckwith for her invaluable assistance in organizing this draft.

Thanks to Terry Nemeth at TCG and to the obsessive and care-giving editor, Steve Samuels.

Finally thanks to Jo Bonney, my muse, conscience and love.

subUrbia

Production History

subUrbia received its world premiere in May 1994 as part of the Festival of New American Plays at Lincoln Center Theater (André Bishop, Artistic Director; Bernard Gersten, Executive Producer). It was directed by Robert Falls; the sets were by Derek McLane, the costumes were by Gabriel Berry, the lighting was by Kenneth Posner, the sound was by John Gromada and the fight direction was by David Leong. The cast was:

JEFF	Josh Hamilton
TIM	Tim Guinee
BUFF	Steve Zahn
SOOZE	Martha Plimpton
BEE-BEE	Wendy Hoopes
PONY	Zak Orth
ERICA	Babette Reneé Props
NAZEER "NORMAN"	Firdous E. Bamji
PAKEESA	Samia Shoaib

subUrbia received development and multiple workshop productions leading to its Lincoln Center premiere in 1994, including a production in spring 1991 at Juilliard in New York, directed by the author. The cast was:

JEFF	Jeff Stafford
TIM	C. J. Wilson
BUFF	Brian Kelly
SOOZE	Carrie Preston
BEE-BEE	Lauren Lovett
PONY	Dallas Roberts
ERICA	Nicole Marcks
NAZEER "NORMAN"	Chris McKinney
PAKEESA	Maya Thomas

In 1996, *subUrbia* was made into a feature film by Castle Rock (distributed in 1997 by Warner Brothers). It was directed by Richard Linklater, with a screenplay by Eric Bogosian and production design by Catherine Hardwicke. The cast was:

JEFF	Giovanni Ribisi
TIM	Nicky Katt
BUFF	Steve Zahn
SOOZE	Amie Carey
BEE-BEE	Dina Spybey
PONY	Jayce Bartok
ERICA	Parker Posey
NAZEER "NORMAN"	Ajay Naidu
PAKEESA	Samia Shoaib

This revised version of *subUrbia* was produced in September 2006 at the Second Stage Theatre (Carole Rothman, Artistic Director; Chris Burney, Associate Artistic Director) in New York. It was directed by Jo Bonney; the sets were by Richard Hoover, the costumes were by Mimi O'Donnell, the lighting was by David Weiner, the sound was by Robert Kaplowitz and the fight direction was by Rick Sordelet. The cast was:

JEFF	Daniel Eric Gold
TIM	Peter Scanavino
BUFF	Kieran Culkin
SOOZE	Gaby Hoffman
BEE-BEE	Halley Feiffer
PONY	Michael Esper
ERICA	Jessica Capshaw
NAZEER "NORMAN"	Manu Narayan
PAKEESA	Diksha Basu

Characters

JEFF GALLAGHER	
TIM MITCHUM	Jeff's best friend, air force vet
BUFF MACLEOD	their friend
SOOZE BECKWITH	Jeff's girlfriend
BEE-BEE DOUGLASS	Sooze's best friend
NEIL "PONY" MOYNIHAN	the group's classmate from high school
ERICA GERSON	Pony's publicist
NAZEER "NORMAN" CHAUDRY	owner of the convenience store
PAKEESA CHAUDRY	his sister

All characters are around twenty.

Setting

Suburban Burnfield, USA

Time

The present

Act One

The house is black. Loud music surges, getting louder.

The music cuts out as the lights come up on the sidewalk along the side of a 7-Eleven-type convenience store. It is an early summer evening. We can see the store interior. A pay phone is on the outside front wall. A small bench lines the same wall. Behind the store, against the rear wall, is a large ice machine. The area stretching out toward the audience and into the wings is asphalt pavement, demarked with yellow parking lines. A large cement curb sits along the extreme downstage edge.

Tim Mitchum, twenty-one years old, is sitting on the sidewalk near the phone, his back to the wall, drinking a beer, smoking a cigarette. His hair is short and his T-shirt reveals an athletic body. Next to him are two pairs of rollerblades, a pair of sneakers and what's left of a six-pack. Propped against the wall are three hockey sticks and a puck.

Nazeer "Norman" Chaudry, twenty-four, and his sister Pakeesa, twenty, can be seen at work within the convenience store. He's at the counter, reading a book as he eats something from a bowl. She's in traditional Pakistani dress, wiping down the cooler cases.

Loud music is heard coming from a boombox as Buff Macleod (on rollerblades, balancing the boombox) and Jeff Gallagher enter, each holding a slice of pizza. Both are about twenty years old. Buff affects a loose "homey" style, while Jeff is simply dressed in dark clothing of no particular style. His hair is messy as if he just woke up.

Buff snaps off the boombox and deposits it on the sidewalk, continuing to roll around in circles as they talk.

BUFF *(To Tim)*: Hey you! Get a job!
JEFF *(Regarding the pizza)*: This is fucking hot.
BUFF: Drip the grease off, man! The grease is the main problem!

> *(Jeff tries to nibble the slice. He takes a big bite and burns his tongue. The slice slips to the ground.)*

JEFF: AAAHHHHH! MOTHERFUCKER-COCKSUCKING-SHIT-SHIT-SHIT!

> *(Jeff stomps his slice with his boot.)*

BUFF: The slice is no match for the kung-fu master!

> *(Jeff jogs into the convenience store. Buff skates near Tim.)*

There was this show on the other day about Asia and shit. They had these Tibetan dudes, man. Like how they pray and do their thing. They just like sit on pillows for hours. And they do this weird singing:

> *(Buff proceeds to make this outlandish nasal droning sound, with surprising expertise, mimicking the Tibetan monks.*
>
> *Jeff grabs a bag of Oreos and a six-pack at the store. He drops some bills on the counter and exits the store.*
>
> *Nazeer, still eating, follows Jeff out.)*

NAZEER *(With a Pakistani accent)*: Hey! $7.20!
JEFF: Huh?
NAZEER: $7.20!
JEFF: I gave it to you!
BUFF *(Skating toward them)*: He paid you, man!
NAZEER: You owe me twenty cents. $7.20! 7.20!
BUFF: Yo! You're spitting rice all over me!

> *(Jeff reaches into his pocket and hands twenty cents to Nazeer, who reenters the store. Jeff sits down on the bench.)*

JEFF: Guy should cut down on the caffeine.
BUFF: Needs some pizza in his diet.

> *(Buff skates past Tim.)*

TIM: Somebody should crack his dot head with a baseball bat. And remove the skates, moron, before I shove 'em up your ass.
BUFF: Fascist! You're a fascist, man!
JEFF: Neo-fascist.
BUFF: Neo-fascist! *Gay* neo-fascist!
TIM: Sit down, you're embarrassing me.
JEFF: The guy's just nervous. Stranger in a strange land. It's gotta be hard.
BUFF: Yesterday I caught him practicing the Pledge of Allegiance. Boning up for the big test: "I pledge allegiance to the flag of the United States of America, and to the Republic . . . and to the Republic, one nation under God, invisible and with justice and mercy for all!"
JEFF: You forgot "liberty." And it's "indivisible," not "invisible."
BUFF: I know it better than he does.
TIM: Of course you do. He has no right.
JEFF: Of course he has a right. He's trying to improve his situation. That's the American way. He's from a third-world country. I respect him for that.

TIM: Spare me that "third-world" shit.

JEFF: That's what you call it.

TIM: I've seen the third world, man. Those places smell like you wiped your ass and made a country out of the paper. The people are dog-eating, greaseballs.

(Buff removes his skates, exchanges them for his sneakers.)

JEFF: He's a human being. You gotta give him that.

TIM: Only thing I gotta give him is a one-way ticket back to greaseball land.

JEFF: He wants to be like us.

TIM: Good luck. We'd get back to base after a weekend in Goa, they'd take our clothes, soak 'em in gasoline just to kill the bugs. Eat an ice cube over there, you get the shits for a week.

JEFF: Those places are screwed-up 'cause we fuck them up.

TIM: What?!! Who's "we"?

JEFF: The American Empire. The air force. You. Me.

TIM: You have no idea what you're talking about. The gooks did it to themselves, pal. Fucking chaos on a stick.

BUFF: But like, isn't that guy from Arabia or some shit like that? You're not a gook if you're from Arabia, man. Gooks are like Chinese and shit.

JEFF: He's from India. The whole family's from India. India and Saudi Arabia aren't even the same continents, jerky!

TIM: The COs used to give us that shit: "Don't confuse the Filipino with the Sri Lankan. Don't confuse the Iraqis with the Indians. It offends them. Don't confuse the Goans with the Schmoans." Bullshit. They're all the same. Sub-human.

(Jeff munches his Oreos, watching Buff eat his pizza.)

JEFF *(Pointing to the pizza on the ground)*: Yeah, well, that pizza could feed a family of four back in India or Armenia or wherever the fuck he comes from.

BUFF: But, how would you ship it, man? Federal Express? By the time it got there it would be way cold and coagulated. Total waste. Cheese would be all stuck to the cardboard.

JEFF: Buffster, that slice you're chomping on could be the difference between life and death for some half-dead Bangladeshi.

BUFF: Yo, homey, you're getting me all upset here.

JEFF: You *should* get upset! Everyone should get upset. When Hitler was greasing the Jews, people were saying, "Don't get me upset! You're bumming me out!" It's my duty as a human being to get pissed off. Not that it makes any difference in the first place. Nothing ever fucking changes. Fifty years from now, we'll all be dead and there'll be new people standing in this same spot drinking beer and eating pizza, bitching and moaning about the price of Oreos, and they won't even know we were ever here. And fifty years after that, those suckers will be dust and bones. And then there will more suckers after them. And all these generations of suckers will try to figure out what the fuck they were doing on this fucking planet and they will all be full of shit. It's all so fucking futile!

TIM: If it's all so fucking futile what the fuck are you so fucking upset about, fuckhead?

JEFF: I'm fucking alienated.

BUFF: Me, too! I'm alienated, too. But at least there's Oreos. *(Grabbing an Oreo)* Oreos, the perfect dessert after the perfect fucking meal! Dark and chocolaty on the outside, white and delicious on the inside. You can eat them whole, or you can split 'em in two, and scrape off the creamy frosting with your teeth.

JEFF: IRAQ! DARFUR! HAITI! You ever watch the news, Buffman? There's a world outside this tar pit of stupidity. But why give a shit? Let's just ignore it. Let's just play in the mud with our iPods. Empty, void, stupid. It's the end of the world, man—no ideas, no hope, no future. The fucking apocalypse. You don't even know what "apocalypse" means, do you, Buff-cake?

BUFF: Of course I do, man. It was a movie. I saw it on cable. Vietnam. Dennis Hopper hanging out with Charlie Sheen's dad. Surfing. Snails crawling on razor blades. "This is the end . . . dum-dum-dum . . . My only friend, the end . . ."

(Tim joins in, preacher-like, as Buff continues to sing the melody under.)

TIM: "And in those days shall men seek death and shall not find it; and shall desire to die, death shall flee from them." John the Seer wrote Apocalypse also known as Revelation. Check your Bible.

BUFF: My mom bought this toilet paper with Christian sayings printed on it, but I told her like if the pope came by for a cup of coffee and had to take a shit we'd all get excommunicated and sent to hell.

JEFF: Yeah, yeah, it's all a big joke. It's because of the pope that the world is crawling with starving people. Ever heard of the slums of Rio?

TIM: Rio? What about Calcutta?

JEFF: Huh?

TIM: Calcutta's pretty overpopulated. Don't think the pope had much to do with that.

JEFF: Well, that's an exception.

TIM: Is it? What about China? About a billion starving non-Christians there in China.

JEFF: So what's your point?

TIM: What's *your* point?

JEFF: Forget it. I'm just saying . . .

TIM: Yeah?

JEFF: Things are fucked-up and no one cares.

TIM: Things are fine with me. How are things with you, Buff?

BUFF *(Happily munching)*: Excellent.

JEFF: Fuck the pope! One half of the world is starving to death, and the other half is hooked up to the internet and their cable TV, absorbing nonstop porno and violence, sucking down high-cholesterol food-fat, getting larger and larger and larger like a bunch of Christmas geese, ultimately bursting with cancer and bad karma.

TIM: "Christmas geese"? Where the fuck did that come from?

JEFF: They force-feed geese to make goose liver pate. We're turning into geese. That's what I'm saying, obviously.

TIM: You learn this at Carver Community College? Took a course in decadence? "Decadence 101."

JEFF: No man, I learned it on Sesame Street. They jammed a funnel down Big Bird and pounded the granola down his gizzard.

BUFF: Every morning while I'm doing my abs I check out Sesame Street. There's this babe on the show, she's like a total fox. Saw her on a porn site.

JEFF: An actress on Sesame Street is on a porn site? What's her name?

BUFF: "Tiffany," "Brianna." I don't know, man! I saw it, with my own dick. There's this website, I charge it to my mom's phone? Unlimited porn links. Surf the net with one hand, choke the chicken with the other. Hey, speaking of choking the chicken, guess who I saw at the mall yesterday? "The Duck."

JEFF: "The Duck"?

BUFF: Remember? The guy who could blow himself.

JEFF: Oh God, right! What was he doing at the mall? Still blowing himself?

BUFF: Giving out *pamphlets*, man. He's a yoga instructor now.

JEFF: Shit!

(Tim smiles for the first time.)

TIM: Fuck!

JEFF: Remember Fred Pierce? Buff says he's gay now.

TIM: Fred Pierce was the best running back we had, no way is he a fag.

BUFF: Yeah, well he isn't running anymore. He's in Mercy Memorial. Something's wrong with him.

JEFF: Tim, didn't you kick his ass one time?

TIM: It was nothing. I lost a tooth, he took a couple of stitches. Fred Pierce is not gay. No one who can run like that is a 'mo.

BUFF: I'm telling ya, man. Donnie was in town and Pierce tried to pick him up in a bar. Didn't know Donnie was from Burnfield. Wanted to go to a hotel room!

(Beat.)

TIM: What's he doing in the hospital?

BUFF: I don't know, man. He moved back home and now he's in the hospital.

TIM: You think you know your friends. Pierce! One more loser.

JEFF: How is Pierce a loser?

TIM: Weak and stupid.

JEFF: Being gay has nothing to do with being weak. Or stupid. A lot of geniuses are gay. Sometimes I wish *I* was gay. It would make my life simpler.

(Buff does pushups.)

BUFF: Stop staring at my butt, dude!

JEFF: Hey, *dude*, homosexuals get laid a lot more than straight normal people. That's all they do is get laid. Must be nice—you want to poke someone, you just say, "Yo, want to get poked?" "Sure do!" "OK, let's go!"

TIM: Oh! My fantasy!

JEFF: You don't have to be with one person all the time, don't have to always be worrying about what they *think*, what they *want*. You're free. To do what *you* want.

TIM: Trouble with the little lady, Jeffrey?

JEFF: I didn't say that. That's not my point.

BUFF: Hey, Jeff, how's Sooze?

TIM: Yes, Jeff, how's Sooze?

JEFF: Who brought up Sooze? No one.

TIM: You did.

JEFF: I did not.

TIM: Sooze is too good for you, Jeff. That's the problem. A man should never be with a woman whose vocabulary is larger than his.

JEFF: My . . . then that must be why you're stuck by yourself.

TIM: Oh, snap! The greats always stand alone, young grasshopper.

BUFF: How's her friend?

JEFF: Which friend?

BUFF: What's-her-name: "Bee-Bee." She's got a nice smile, that Bee-Bee.

JEFF: She's gonna be here later, ask her yourself.

BUFF: OK. So I'm at work yesterday, bitch comes in, orders a twelve-inch pie with extra cheese. I ask her if she wanted me to like carry it out to her vehicle . . . right? Bitch is obviously in heat. Says, "Yes," right away. So I carry the pie out to her car. We end up smoking a jay, we eat the pizza, I chase it with a beer. Then she blows me. Smoke, slice, brew, babe—all four food groups, man.

(Jeff takes out his cell phone and walks away from the other two.)

JEFF: Buff, your ability to fantasize is only exceeded by your ability to lie.

(Buff follows Jeff as he hits autodial.)

BUFF: Untrue, Jeffster. Last week I picked up two horny nymphets at the Chili Peppers concert. Two on one. I swear. You can ask them. I got their numbers.

(Listening to his phone, Jeff makes a jerk-off motion with his hand.)

TIM: Fuckin' Pierce. I knew something was wrong with him. Must have been why we blew the playoffs.

JEFF *(Into the phone)*: It's me. I'm down the store. With Tim and Buff. Nothing. What about, you know "the plan"? . . . What about your mother's car? Oh. So pick me up and we'll meet him somewhere. What did he say?

(Buff turns on the boombox, loud. He picks up a hockey stick and starts fucking with Tim. Tim grabs the stick. They start wrestling as Jeff continues to talk on his phone.)

(Into the phone) Did you tell him we aren't going because the tickets were too expensive? Ever hear of a comp list? . . . Sooze, there's always a comp list.

(Nazeer emerges from the store.)

NAZEER: Hey, you guys! You can't be out here all night tonight.

(Buff and Tim ignore him. Norman walks over and turns off the boombox.)

BUFF: We're just having a conversation.

JEFF *(Into the phone)*: So what's the deal? . . . Why? . . . we're just supposed to hang around until he shows up? That's harder. Why can't you . . . All right. All right. I said all right. Drive over here and we'll switch to my dad's Cherokee.

NAZEER: This is private property.

BUFF: Hey, this is America, man, don't tell us about private property, OK?

NAZEER: You gotta go now! The customers complain.

BUFF: *We're* your customers, man. We're not complaining.
NAZEER: Please!

(Buff turns the boombox on again. He and Tim get into an almost absurd slam-dance.
Nazeer watches for a second, then turns the boombox off once more.
Jeff hangs up and turns on Nazeer.)

JEFF: I was talking to my mother who is in the hospital dying of terminal cancer, that OK with you?
NAZEER: So go visit her if she's in hospital.
BUFF: You dissin' his mother, man?

(Pakeesa, from within the store, taps on the window. She holds up a portable phone.)

PAKEESA *(In Urdu):* Nazeer, for you, Hassan.

(Nazeer turns from them and reenters the store. When he takes the phone from Pakeesa his demeanor goes easy. Laughing, he keeps an eye on Tim, Buff and Jeff.)

TIM: Who you talking to?
JEFF: Nobody. Sooze.
BUFF: Sooze coming down?
JEFF *(Bending over to tie his shoe):* Maybe. Uh . . . it's my birthday. This week. She's coming by to wish me happy birthday.
BUFF: Your birthday? Well, shit!

(Jeff's still bent over as Buff grabs him by the rump and starts "humping him.")

"HAPPY BIRTHDAY TO YOU! HAPPY BIRTHDAY TO YOU!"

(This starts a mock fight. Buff keeps singing throughout. Tim joins in, humping Buff. The three hurtle around the parking lot locked in a bizarre mock-fuck fight.)

BUFF AND TIM: "HAPPY BIRTHDAY, DEAR JEFFY! HAPPY BIRTH-DAY TO YOU!"

(Bee-Bee Douglass enters. The cluster-fight barrels into Bee-Bee then breaks apart.)

BEE-BEE: Hey! Watch it, asshole!

JEFF: He's the asshole!

(Bee-bee sits on the bench and lights a cigarette.)

BEE-BEE: What did Sooze say? Is Pony coming?

JEFF: I don't know.

(Buff sidles up to Bee-Bee.)

BUFF: Wanna beer?

BEE-BEE: Uh, I don't drink. What did she say? Did she talk to Pony?

TIM: "Pony"? "Pony"? What's a "pony"? Not that geek who played folk music at the senior prom?

JEFF: Neil Moynihan.

TIM: God!

BUFF: Pony's band, Cat's Cradle's been on tour opening for Midnight Whore. Stadiums, man! So, Pony's coming by here?

BEE-BEE *(To Tim)*: Didn't you see their video on MTV?

TIM: I shot my TV.

BUFF: So, Pony's coming by?

JEFF: And anyway, now's he's back and we thought maybe we'd get together tonight. And, you know, talk. That's all. No big deal. Me, him and Sooze . . .

TIM: Uh-huh. You wanted to get together with your close friend: Neil the rock star? Sure, I understand. You want us to leave?

JEFF: No. We're gonna go someplace or something.

BEE-BEE: We are?

JEFF: She told him to come here. Fuck.

BUFF: Pony's coming?

JEFF: Don't ask me, ask Sooze.

TIM: If you want to be alone with Neil, Jeff, it's all right with us.

JEFF: It was just something we were going to do.

TIM: No, I mean, you two should be alone together. Talk about old times. Have some laughs. Warm your hands by the fire. Bond.

BUFF: When?

JEFF: It's not like that. I don't give a shit.

TIM: Sure you do.

JEFF: I don't even like his music that much. But we were friends.

TIM: When were you friends?

JEFF: Sooze wants to see him.

TIM: Oh, *I* want to see him, too!

BUFF: We *all* want to see him. When is he coming?

BEE-BEE: Yeah, when's he coming?

JEFF: Later.

(Blackout. Lights up on Sooze standing in front of the wall sipping from a takeout container of coffee. Jeff, Tim, Buff and Bee-Bee are sitting on crates, the curb, etc., watching Sooze perform.)

SOOZE: (1) I look into the mirror, what do I see? Eyes, tits, teeth, cunt. Smile baby smile. You're here for a purpose. Where's the fertilizer? (2) I stick a knife in my hand, what do I see? Blood. Red and sticky as anybody else's. Any man. Any African-American's. Any slave's. I bang my head, what do I hear? Silence. (3) Fuck the president. Fuck the vice-president. Fuck the secretary of defense. Fuck the secretary of *offense*. Fuck the pope. Fuck my dad. Fuck the men. Fuck the men. Fuck all the men. (4) What is a male's *good time*?

A piece of ass. A hard ball. A porno tape. A hamburger with ketchup and sperm spread all over it.

BUFF: Yummy!

SOOZE *(Losing her place)*: Oh shit.

BEE-BEE: "What are you looking at?"

SOOZE: Oh yeah. (5) Hey what are you looking at? You want some of this? You like this? Hear you go. *(Spreads her legs, shows her butt)* Here's the hole. Jump on in. Or do you just want to look? (6) Bang your head, blow your nose, run down the street, suck a hose / Chew my lips, eat some shit, eat a stick of dynamite and blow yourself to bits / Shut your mouth, go away, drink my piss, have a nice day / I hope you cry and never doubt I hope you die with blood in your mouth, I hope your lies will no more shout what's in my eyes what's in your snout / You are a pig I know that's true / I dance a jig fuck you fuck you fuck you fuck you fuck you!

(She finishes.)

Slides go with it. Behind me.

JEFF: Is that supposed to be about me?

BEE-BEE: It's called "Burger Manifesto: Part I—The Dialectical Exposition of Testosterone." Isn't that the best title?

JEFF: Is that supposed to be about me?

BEE-BEE: I'm making the slides.

SOOZE: Why is everything about you, Jeff?

JEFF: Not everything. This. I *am* the man in your life.

SOOZE: "Man"?

JEFF: Yeah, "man," "male," "significant other," whatever the fuck I am.

TIM: Phallic symbol.

JEFF: Phallic symbol. *(Thinks)* No.

SOOZE: It's a piece!

JEFF *(Walking away)*: A piece.

SOOZE: So, do you think it's good?

TIM: I think it's great. When are you taking it on the road?

SOOZE: I'm not actually doing it anywhere, I'm just composing it as part of my application to the School of Visual Arts . . . in New York.

BUFF: Sooze, you know people in New York?

SOOZE: No. I'll just go. *(Pause)* I figure the worst I could do is starve to death.

JEFF: "The worst I could do is starve to death." Listen to you!

SOOZE: I don't want to hear it.

JEFF: Because you haven't a fucking clue! You're all ready to pack your bags and leap into the unknown because some conceptual artist who teaches at a community college is having a mid-life crisis and wants to sleep with a girl half his age, so he tells you you have "talent."

SOOZE: Mr. Brooks is not a "conceptual artist." He's a site-specific performance studies instructor. He's had shows in New York. He knows. He had a review in *Artforum* magazine.

JEFF: He's in a *magazine*! Well, then you better listen to him.

SOOZE: Fuck. Might as well not do anything. No one should do anything. Let's just stick our thumbs up our ass and twirl!

TIM *(Applauding):* Bravo. Go to New York and make art, Sooze. They need you. They need your unique point of view.

SOOZE: At least I *have* a point of view. I stand for something. I am trying to communicate something.

TIM: That's right. You are.

JEFF *(To Sooze):* What are you trying to communicate? Tell us.

SOOZE: So you can give me more shit?

JEFF: I'm asking an honest question. What are you trying to communicate?

SOOZE: I am trying to communicate how I feel. You know? Raise consciousness. Make people think for a change.

JEFF: About *what*?

SOOZE: About things that are important to me. Sexual politics, racism, global warming. Things!

BEE-BEE: Violence against women.

SOOZE: Yeah.

JEFF: Racism? You don't even know anybody who's black!

SOOZE: Of course I do!

JEFF: Name one.

SOOZE: Karen Johnson.

JEFF: One.

SOOZE: You completely miss the point. I'm talking about idealism!

BEE-BEE: Responsibility! Progress!

JEFF: Idealism is guilty, middle-class bullshit.

SOOZE: *Cynicism* is bullshit.

JEFF: I'm not being cynical. I'm being honest.

SOOZE: But do you stand for anything? What? What do *you* stand for?

TIM: Go get 'em, Sooze.

JEFF: I stand for honesty. Some level of . . .

SOOZE: Yeah, right.

JEFF: Let me talk!

BEE-BEE: What a dildo!

SOOZE: Fuck you.

BEE-BEE: Go eat an Oreo.

SOOZE: Yeah go eat an Oreo.

JEFF: What's so funny about that?

SOOZE: All you know is what's good for you, Jeff. Typical male.

JEFF: Can I talk? Can I make a point here?

BEE-BEE: No.

SOOZE: Tim, on an objective level. Seriously. Do you think it's a good idea?

TIM: It's a good idea.

SOOZE: Thank you. See, he did it. He left. He got his ass out of here. Now it's my turn.

TIM: I did. I expanded my horizons. I served my country, and I saw the world. I sowed my wild oats. And now I'm back. I've gained wisdom and now I'm back. Go, you have my blessing, child.

SOOZE: Where's Pony? Be nice to have a conversation with a human being.

BUFF: I'm an independent filmmaker. I been making these tapes. I ripped off a camcorder up at the mall and I've been making these tapes. I thought, it could be, you know, something I *do*. Like I was walking around my house and—

TIM: Buff, the postmodern idiot savant! He will outdo us all!

JEFF: Since when did you get this big affection for "Pony"? You didn't even know him in school.

SOOZE: Of course I did! He sat right behind me in study hall. All we did was talk. He called *me*, remember?

JEFF: You used to make fun of him.

SOOZE: I did not. Now you're lying.

JEFF: If you love him so much, why didn't you go see him play?

SOOZE: Because you didn't want to pay for the tickets.

JEFF: I'm not going to pay forty-five bucks to see Neil Moynihan play in a band *I* helped start.

SOOZE: He's always been a nice guy and I like him.

JEFF AND TIM: He's a geek.

(Sooze turns on the boombox, loud. Nazeer comes out of the store, a broom in his hand.)

NAZEER: That's it, that's it. I'm calling the police!

JEFF: We're just standing here!

NAZEER: You are trespassing.

BUFF: Call the cops, man. Call 'em right now! Maybe my cousin Jerry will show up. He'll definitely take your word against mine. You tell him about the trespassing, and I'll tell him about how you sell cigarettes to minors. We'll see who spends the night in jail.

NAZEER: I'm not joking now. Let's go!

SOOZE: We're just standing here!

(Pakeesa watches from inside the store. She disappears into the back of the store.)

NAZEER: Go stand someplace else.

BUFF: *You* stand someplace else, man! You stand someplace else. This is our spot. You don't fucking own it.

NAZEER: Yes, I do. I *do* own it. It's mine. And you don't belong here.

BUFF: *You* don't belong here, man. We were here before you.

TIM: Why don't you just go back to where you come from?

SOOZE: Tim!

TIM: What? You standing up for this guy? Fuckin' camel jockey.

NAZEER: And what are you, you drunk! You just hang around . . . on my property!

(Tim steps into Nazeer.)

TIM: Fuck you. You want us to go? Do something.

(Nazeer turns away. Tim quickly cuts him off.)

SOOZE: Jeff!

(Jeff does nothing.)

Tim, you win, you have the biggest penis, can we go now?

(Nazeer puts his hand on Tim's shoulder to get past him. Tim grabs Nazeer's arm. He whirls Nazeer around, throwing him.)

TIM: Don't you fuckin' touch me!

(Tim pushes Nazeer hard. Nazeer stumbles even more. Jeff jumps in to separate them.)

JEFF: Hey! Hey! Hey!

(Buff holds Jeff back.)

BUFF: Let 'em, fight. The dude wants it.
SOOZE: No! Hey, wait a minute! This is getting ridiculous.

(Nazeer clutches his broomstick defensively.)

NAZEER: OK, OK. I'm not afraid of you, you drunken shit.
BEE-BEE: Tim, let's go. You're gonna hurt the guy!
NAZEER: Good for nothing!

(Tim grabs the hockey stick from Buff.)

SOOZE: Tim, what are you doing!? Stop it! Jeff!!!

(Jeff does nothing.)

TIM: You want to be an American? You should learn a sport!
(Feints two or three hockey moves to an imaginary puck) This
is called "hockey."

*(Suddenly Tim steps forward, "moving the puck"; he "checks"
Nazeer hard. Nazeer falls backward onto the pavement. He
tries to fend off Tim with the broom. Tim tries to tug the broom
away from him.)*

Hey, don't start crying now!

*(Nazeer crawls backward to get away from Tim as Tim hits the
ground hard around him, chasing him. Then Pakeesa emerges
from the store, holding a .38-special.)*

PAKEESA *(In Urdu)***:** Haramzadeh, madarachot. Seewer ka baacha!
(Filthy bastard, motherfucker. Son of a pig!)
SOOZE: Oh, shit!

TIM: What's this? Your mother?

NAZEER: It's OK, Pakeesa. *(Pause)* Pakeesa, it's OK. Go back in the store. Go back.

PAKEESA *(In Urdu)*: You come in, too.

BUFF: Yo, mama, that thing loaded?

BEE-BEE: Let's go!

NAZEER *(To Pakeesa)*: In a minute.

PAKEESA *(In Urdu)*: Nazeer, don't be crazy now.

(Nazeer stands and brushes himself off.)

BUFF: Tim, you think she's got bullets in that thing?

NAZEER *(In Urdu)*: Come on, Pakeesa. It's OK. *(In English)* They're just joking around.

TIM: Pull the trigger, bitch.

BUFF: Yeah, we were just screwing around. Like Muhammad said. Can't take a joke, man. *(To Pakeesa)* I hope you got a permit for that, mama.

PAKEESA *(In Urdu)*: I'm going to call the police.

NAZEER *(In English)*: No police.

SOOZE: We're sorry, we'll go.

(Pakeesa moves toward the store, followed by Nazeer. Tim follows, taunting her.)

TIM: Somebody pulls a gun, they should know what to do with it.

SOOZE: Come on, Bee-Bee, let's get away from these racist, macho-fixated assholes.

(Bee-Bee starts to exit with Sooze. Buff grabs the hockey sticks.)

TIM: Kill or be killed, comprende? You're gonna regret this, you brown bitch.

BUFF: Fuck her. Let's go. Find some weed.

(Sooze and Bee-Bee exit. Nazeer steers Pakeesa back into the store. He turns and stands in the doorway.)

PAKEESA *(In Urdu)*: Nazeer, come inside.

(Tim turns to go with Buff, then stops and walks up to Nazeer, taunts him a little. Then they leave.
Jeff makes a show of picking up some of their trash.)

JEFF: Hey, man, I'm sorry . . . OK? He's drunk.
BUFF *(From offstage)*: FUCKING DOTHEAD!
JEFF: It's a misunderstanding. He's upset about something and he took it out on you.

(Nazeer turns to face him.)

I'm not . . . I don't want to hurt you. I'm on your side, man. Really.

(Nazeer turns from Jeff and goes into the store. As Jeff walks off, music comes up loud.)

Act Two

Lights up. The store is closed and dark.

Bee-Bee is standing alone, eyes closed, nodding her head and dancing to the music of the boombox.

Tim enters, sees Bee-Bee, then climbs to the roof.

Buff enters, sits on the bench and watches Bee-Bee. She pauses when she sees him. Buff closes his eyes and nods his head to the music. Bee-Bee resumes her "dance." Both are moving to the beat, apart, yet together.

The song ends. Bee-Bee approaches Buff and sits next to him.

BUFF: Hey.
BEE-BEE: Hey. Gimme a cigarette?

> (Buff gives Bee-Bee a cigarette. He lights it. They smoke in silence.)

> You made a film?

BUFF: What?

BEE-BEE: Nothin'.

BUFF: What?

BEE-BEE: You said you made a video. What's it about?

BUFF: It's not about anything.

BEE-BEE: Oh. What's on it?

BUFF: Stuff I got off the TV. *The Jetsons.* And some shit blowing up I saw on the news. Plus one day my mom was praying and shit and she didn't see me watching and I videotaped her.

BEE-BEE: Yeah? Your mom praying?

(Beat.)

BUFF: And a cloud.

BEE-BEE: A cloud?

BUFF: There was this cloud and I videotaped it.

BEE-BEE: Oh.

BUFF: I was doing 'shrooms and I saw this cloud. It looks excellent on the tape. It's like, the video is my head? And everything, you know, is like in there that I see. My moms and TV and the sky and plus I'm going to come down here one night and walk around inside the store with the camera. Tape shit.

BEE-BEE: That would be amazing.

BUFF: Yeah. Like imagine the inside of the store but with music. I'll add music—Sonic Youth . . .

BEE-BEE: Yes!

BUFF: System of a Down, White Stripes . . .

BEE-BEE: Barry Manilow . . .

BUFF: Uh . . . yeah. Yeah!

BEE-BEE: Yeah?

BUFF: Plus, one night when nobody noticed I taped everybody talking, you know? So I'm putting some of that shit in, too.

BEE-BEE: Cool.

(Beat.)

What did I say?

BUFF: Uh. Nothin'. You know?

BEE-BEE: I wish I could see it. Your video.

BUFF: You can see it. Whenever you want.

BEE-BEE: Yeah?

BUFF *(Direct)*: Sure.

(Bee-Bee gets up and paces near the bench.)

Don't you work at a hospital or something?

BEE-BEE: Yeah. I'm a nurse's aide at Mercy.

BUFF: You're a nurse?

BEE-BEE: No. I, you know, clean 'em up. Empty the bedpans. Sometimes I feed 'em their lunch. That kind of thing.

BUFF: Old people? Like with Alzheimer's? Really fucked-up?

BEE-BEE: Some of 'em. Strokes. A lot of types I don't know what's wrong with 'em. They're not moving too much and they get kind of yellow. Usually they die if they're real yellow.

(Buff paces like Bee-Bee.)

BUFF: Sounds like a total bummer.

BEE-BEE: No, it's not. I like it. I mean they're not all completely, you know, in a *coma*. They're happy that I'm helping 'em. Fred Pierce? He's there. He's going blind. I guess it's AIDS? We just had a birthday party for him last week. Doctor Patel says he'll die pretty soon. But Fred's great to talk to. Fucking funny guy. Says things like: "Watch it or I'll bleed on you."

(They sit on the ground.)

BUFF: Fred's going to die?

BEE-BEE: Well, you know, he's really sick.

BUFF: I thought there were drugs for that now?

BEE-BEE: Not always. Depends.

BUFF: Oh, doesn't that, like, bother you?

BEE-BEE: Sure, but it's a lot worse for him. I know he needs me, you know, just to say hi and talk. I need him.

BUFF: Yeah, yeah. That's good, I guess.

(Buff leans back into the curb. Beat. Bee-Bee sits the same way. Buff speaks to the sky.)

What are you doing now?

BEE-BEE: Right now?

BUFF: Yeah.

BEE-BEE: Waiting, I guess. This whole thing with Neil, I mean, Pony—Sooze is pretty excited. Maybe he'll have a stretch limo or something. I dunno. I think it's stupid.

BUFF: No, I know what you mean. *(Pause)* Wanna go out back, in the woods?

BEE-BEE: Now?

BUFF: We could smoke a doob. Hang out.

BEE-BEE: I don't do drugs. *(Pause)* But I'll go back. OK?

BUFF: Whatever you want.

(Tentatively they both stand. Bee-Bee takes the boombox. Buff takes her hand and they exit behind the store into the woods.

Tim, on the roof, sets an empty beer can on the edge, and lightly blows it off.

Jeff and Sooze enter arguing.)

SOOZE: It was a racial incident!

JEFF: It was just something that got out of hand! It isn't like Tim was going to hurt the guy.

SOOZE: He pushed him!

JEFF: And *they* pulled out a gun. Did you see that? What's that about? In the end, did anyone get hurt?

SOOZE: Yeah!

JEFF: Believe me, if I thought anything really bad was going to happen, I would have done something.

SOOZE: Yeah? What would you have done?

JEFF: I would have stopped it.

SOOZE: How?

JEFF: I would have done something. This is kind of hypothetical isn't it?

> *(Drawing Sooze to him)* Hey. Can we drop this for two minutes? I haven't seen you all day.

(They kiss. Jeff holds her close, kissing her neck.)

> No one's here. Let's go around back to the van.

SOOZE: Not the van! It smells in there . . . Yech! Moldy old blankets, beer cans . . . there's enough stuff stuck to the floor to open a sperm bank!

JEFF: Then let's take a ride up to the field.

SOOZE: Pony's coming. Can't you just hold me for a minute.

(A moment passes.)

> I went by my sister's this afternoon.

JEFF: Yeah?

SOOZE: Jerry was outside lighting the barbecue and Debbie's in the kitchen making macaroni salad.

> I'm watching Michelle in her crib and Jerry Junior on the shag carpet watching TV and I suddenly felt like I couldn't breathe.

JEFF: Why?

SOOZE: Because Debbie's like this stranger. This "mom." And she treats me like I'm a kid. Like she's mature and I'm not. Like she knows something I don't . . .

JEFF: Don't compare yourself with your sister. You have a life. You're going to school. You're an artist, she's a housewife married to a guy who installs vinyl siding.

(Sooze shifts so she can sit and face Jeff.)

SOOZE: I was talking to Mr. Brooks yesterday, he has this friend in New York who wants to sublet his apartment. Nine hundred a month.

JEFF: Yeah?

SOOZE: I could swing that, nine hundred.

JEFF: Sooze.

SOOZE: What?

JEFF: There's more to it than getting an apartment.

SOOZE: But that's major.

JEFF: No, I mean—yes. But did it ever occur to you that I might have some feelings about you moving to New York?

SOOZE: What feelings?

JEFF: Us.

SOOZE: Of course!

JEFF: And?

SOOZE: Come with me!

JEFF: No! See that's not what I'm saying. *(Walks away from her)*

SOOZE: Well, what *are* you saying?

JEFF: I could go to New York if I wanted to. But what's the point? So I can learn how to hail a cab? So I can get mugged by some crack-head? So I can see raggedy homeless people up close?

SOOZE: Maybe you *should* see "raggedy homeless people up close."

JEFF: That's stupid.

SOOZE: So what do you want to do?

JEFF: Nothing.

SOOZE: No one does nothing, Jeff.

JEFF *(Defiant)*: I'm going to break new ground.

SOOZE: "New ground"? Taking one community college course on the history of Cuba, while barely holding a job packing boxes?

JEFF: My job is not who I am. I don't need that to define myself.

SOOZE: So what do you need?

JEFF: Nothing. Jobs. Things. Stuff. I don't need any of that. Too many possessions clutter your brain.

SOOZE: You find that in a fortune cookie?

JEFF: Tim said it actually.

(Beat.)

Did you know that when Tim got out of the service, he hitchhiked from here to San Francisco and back? *Alone?*

SOOZE: Well, golly! Hitchhiker, Air Force dropout, corner bum, racist. My hero. Jeff, he's just some guy hanging out. You act like he's God.

JEFF: Because he knows. Because he's been there.

SOOZE: He's an alcoholic loser.

JEFF: And what am I?

SOOZE: Jeff, you're . . .

JEFF: All I want to do is make something that shatters the world. If I can't do that, I don't want to do anything.

SOOZE: That's so egotistical.

JEFF: Yeah? What's your goal? Getting reviewed in an art magazine? Getting your stuff in a gallery? Making thousands of dollars?

SOOZE: My goal is to make my art.

JEFF: So why can't you do that here? What's wrong with here? How is someplace else better?

SOOZE: Why should I stay here, Jeff? So I can sit next to you and watch the lights change while you bitch about Burnfield? So I can spend the rest of my life guessing what it would be like to be a real artist? So you and I can *fuck* while your parents are out having dinner at the Sizzler? I mean, what are we doing? You and me?

JEFF: I don't know. I just want us to be happy. You got this thing about leaving, about New York. But isn't this as good as anyplace? Really? Look, I'm saying it. I don't want you to go away. Who will I talk to? Who will I make love to?

SOOZE: Jeff.

JEFF: Who will I dream with?

SOOZE: You don't have any dreams.

(Buff enters from behind the store, zipping up his fly.)

He's gonna be here soon. We're outta beer. *(She leaves)*

BUFF *(Goes to the pay phone and dials; into the phone)*: Frankie!!! What you doing? Sleeping? Don't sleep! Sleep when you're *dead*, come out! . . . Get your clothes on and come down here, man! I want to see you. Yeah. I miss you, man. And bring that weed you just bought! What? Hello? *(Hangs up; to Jeff)* So the old man let you have the SUV? Excellent. Maybe we'll do some off-roading later.

JEFF: I can't.

BUFF: Why the fuck not?

JEFF: He checks for mud on the tires when I bring it home.

BUFF: Yeah? I know, we'll take Pony's stretch off-road.

JEFF: I seriously doubt Pony has a stretch.

BUFF: Of course he does. With a chauffeur.

JEFF: No way.

BUFF: Bet you money he's in a stretch right now. Little color TV going. One of those minibars with scotch and shit in the crystal bottles. Fresh ice. Nachos. Babes.

JEFF: You should have a checkup. You're delusional.

BUFF: He's a rock star, man. That's the rock star thing. Bet he has a babe with him right out of a triple-X video. *(Mimes a porno actress getting butt-fucked)* Oh! Oh! Oh! Give it to me, Pony, you stud!

JEFF: Dream on.

BUFF: You wanna bet he's with a girl?

JEFF: He's not with a girl. He's not in a limo.

(Buff mimes giving head.)

BUFF: Oh! Oh! Pony, it's so huge! Oh my God! Groupies. All rock stars have groupies.

JEFF: (A) He's not a rock star. (B) He probably gets bored with all that shit.

BUFF: Yeah? How do you figure that?

JEFF: There's a limit to how much partying you can do.

(Bee-Bee enters. She sits on the bench.)

BUFF: No there isn't.

JEFF: I'd get bored.

BUFF: I wouldn't. I'd wake up every morning singing. I'd have a schedule, man. First, do my workout. Then, take a shower, followed by a hearty breakfast of steak and eggs, washed down with a pot of hot coffee and a six-pack of Bud Light. I'd smoke a joint, then I'd order my bodyguard to find my babe who would appear decked out in her all-black, leather Victoria's Secret custom-made bodysuit, so I'd like have to chew all her clothes off until she was completely and totally nude. Except she'd have these amazing dragon tattoos all over her body and pierced nipples with little gold peace signs hanging off 'em. And then she'd pull out this half ounce of blow and we'd snap out these prodigious lines, vaporize a few million brain cells, screw for about an hour, then spend the rest of the morning trashed, watching *American Idol* on TiVo.

JEFF: Yeah, and what would you do in the afternoon?

BUFF: Same. More of the same. I'd just keep doing the same thing round and round the clock with an occasional burger or slice thrown in for vitamins and energy. And instead of *Idol*, we'd watch *ThunderCats*.

JEFF: Sounds depressing.

(Buff sits next to Bee-Bee and puts his arm around her.)

BUFF: Come on, man, tell me you wouldn't love it!

JEFF: I'm not saying I wouldn't love it. I'm saying after a while it would wear thin.

BUFF: A long while. A long, long while. A long, long, long, long while!

JEFF: What's this? Romance?

BUFF: We're exploring possibilities. Hey, you got any grass?

JEFF: No.

BUFF *(Standing)*: I've got this sudden urge to visit Frankie. *(To Bee-Bee)* You comin'?

(Buff and Bee-Bee exit. Jeff is alone once more. He wanders off behind the store to pee.)

PONY *(From offstage)*: Sooze? Yo, anybody here?

(Jeff hears him, but since he's in the middle of his pee, he doesn't stop to yell out.
　　Neil "Pony" Moynihan enters carrying a guitar.)

Yo?

(Jeff comes around from the back of the store.)

JEFF: Hey!

PONY: Oh, hey, man.

JEFF: Pony!

PONY: Jeff?

(Jeff approaches Pony and embraces him.)

Jeff! Wow.

JEFF: Look at you!

PONY *(Scanning the area)*: You alone?

JEFF: Not anymore. Uh. Wanna beer?

PONY: Sure.

> *(Jeff passes a beer to Pony and takes one for himself. Pony waves to someone. Jeff follows his look.)*

JEFF: That's your limo, huh?

PONY: The record company makes me use it. It's bizarre.

JEFF: I wouldn't know, never been in one.

PONY: I'll give you a ride later. So you're just here alone?

JEFF: They went to get refreshments.

PONY: Sooze?

JEFF: She's here. She'll be here.

PONY: You and her still . . . ?

JEFF: Yeah.

PONY: That's good. That's important. She's so great. *(Looks around)* Wow, man. This town. Nothing's changed!

JEFF: You've only been gone a year. So they give you a limo, huh?

PONY: Yeah. The driver knows Billy Joel. Wow, huh?

JEFF: Heh, that's funny. I saw your album at Musicland up the mall.

PONY: Yeah, we're starting to get good placement. We've sold over ninety thousand units. Danny says we're gonna get a gold record.

JEFF: Gold record, huh? Must be great. Living the wild life, huh?

PONY: No . . .

JEFF: Rock star. Fame. Fortune. Groupies.

PONY: Groupies, right. It's hard work, man. The road! The road is hell. Airport-hotel-show-airport-hotel-show-airport-hotel-show. Still living at your mom's?

JEFF: I just crash there. A lot of nights I'm just out. You know.

PONY: Sure. I saw your dad's SUV parked out front so I knew you were here.

(Erica Gerson enters talking on a cell phone. Erica is a dark beauty, with sophisticated hair and makeup. She carries and fixates on a Blackberry.)

ERICA: Uh-huh, uh-huh, uh-huh. OK. Cool. *(Hangs up; to Pony)* He says "eight A.M."

(Erica finds a seat on the bench and works the Blackberry.)

PONY: Great! Erica, Jeff, Jeff, Erica.

JEFF: Hi.

ERICA: Hi. *So*, uh, is this where we're meeting your friend?

PONY: Yeah, yeah. This is it.

JEFF: So you having any fun, man?

PONY: Some. People are weird, they think you're somebody special if they see you on MTV. You know?

JEFF: Yeah, when you're really just nobody.

PONY: Not "nobody."

JEFF: I mean, just a person.

PONY: It's amazing to be back home. I mean we've been playing big places everywhere, but when we were in the stadium sound-checking, it suddenly hit me. Twenty thousand people, you know? I mean last time I played around here was the prom! *(Laughs)*

ERICA: You played at your prom?

PONY: Yeah. You know.

JEFF: You went kind of nuts that night.

PONY: I thought you guys might come to the show . . .

JEFF: Sooze screwed up the tickets, you know?

PONY: We were pretty good tonight.

ERICA: The band was *amazing* tonight.

PONY: We were?

ERICA: Oh yeah! You *especially*.

PONY: So what's happening with you? How's college?

JEFF: I dropped out. I mean, this semester I'm just taking one class three nights a week. I'm trying to rethink things. You know? Value system, priorities. I read a lot.

(Pony nods sagely. Jeff looks to Erica for some kind of response. She smiles.)

And I'm writing stuff. Short pieces.

ERICA: I *love* writing. Did you read the *Da Vinci Code*? Wasn't it off the hook?

PONY: "Pieces," huh? You should try writing songs.

JEFF: You know, I've thought of that, actually.

PONY: I mean it. You're a good writer. I remember those things you'd write in Mr. Fresher's English class. Funny shit. *(To Erica)* He wrote this thing about his dick once. Read it in front of the whole class.

ERICA: Oh, I'd love to read that!

JEFF: But, so, you think I should?

PONY: What?

JEFF: Write? Because I have. Written some things. You know.

PONY: Songs?

JEFF: They could be songs.

PONY: Yeah? You should show 'em to me.

JEFF: No.

PONY: Really.

JEFF: Now?

PONY: Maybe later.

(Beat.)

JEFF *(Relaxing)*: Hey.

PONY: Hey, you know?

JEFF: I'm thinking, he's out there, he's touring, he's a big deal now. MTV. Stadiums. And then you show up and you're just Pony.

PONY: I'm just Pony, man.

JEFF: Now that I'm thinking about it, it *would* be interesting to do something together.

PONY: It would.

JEFF: Yeah. *(Pause)* You're doing good work, man. You're inspirational.

PONY *(Serious)*: So are you, man.

JEFF: Maybe I'll stop by the house and get the songs later.

PONY: You should.

ERICA: Yeah!

(Sooze enters, hauling bags of beer.)

SOOZE: Didn't want to serve me! Made me show him an ID! I said, "I'm not showing you any fucking ID. You know me, I'm in here every other night!" Fucking long-haired, pot-bellied fifty-something baby-boomer dick-wit.

JEFF: Sooze. *(Indicates the new arrivals)*

SOOZE: Pony! HI!

(She runs up to him and gives him a hug.)

Oh my God. You showed up! Oh, shit! There's your limo! Wow, a real limo. I never saw a black one before.

PONY: It's stupid isn't it?

SOOZE: No, it isn't . . . it's . . . cool.

PONY: Almost got lost on the way!

SOOZE: No! *(Pause)* Pony!!!

PONY: Sooze!!! You look good, Sooze. Like your head's in a good place. Still doing your painting?

SOOZE: Sometimes. I'm starting to do performances. And I don't look good, I look like shit. My head's in a shitty place.
(To Erica) Hi.

ERICA: Hi, I'm Erica.

PONY: "Performances"?

SOOZE: Performance art. You know? Laurie Anderson? Karen Finley? Eve Ensler?

PONY: Oh, yeah. Sure. I met Henry Rollins in L.A.

SOOZE: You did? I like his stuff.

PONY: He's incredible in person. My manager, Danny, took me to this restaurant and there he was.

SOOZE: Wow. He was just sitting there?

PONY: Oh yeah. Just sitting there, eating tofu. That kind of thing happens all the time in L.A. I've met Johnny Depp.

JEFF: Johnny Depp, really?

PONY: You'd like him.

JEFF: No, I wouldn't.

SOOZE: Jeff, how do you know if you would like somebody or not?

ERICA: He seems like a nice guy.

(Jeff sits, distancing himself from the conversation.)

SOOZE: I'm thinking of moving to New York. To go to school. And paint. Performances, paint.

PONY: New York, huh?

SOOZE: Not a good move, huh?

PONY: I think it's a great move. We go through New York all the time and it's the shit. You'd love it there. Plus you always did such great work. You should really take it to the next step. I still have some of those drawings you'd do in study hall.

SOOZE: You do?

PONY: Sure, I saved 'em. Jeff, you gonna go to New York, too?

JEFF: Probably not. I've been pretty busy with my writing.

SOOZE: Jeff isn't into the idea.

PONY: Why not?

JEFF: Well, like I just said, you know, you have to look at the big picture. There's a lot of variables.

PONY: Sure. That's true. But on the other hand . . .

(Buff rushes in with the boombox, breathless. He ducks behind the corner of the building. Bee-Bee follows right after him, laughing.)

BUFF: If the cops roll by, I'm not here!

(Tim hangs over the edge of the roof.)

TIM: What happened?

(Buff cowers behind the dumpster.)

BEE-BEE: Frankie's mom called the cops 'cause Buff was crawling over the roof trying to get to Frankie's room, so he could get some pot.

TIM: Did you succeed?

(Tim hops down to join Buff. Buff triumphantly pulls out a small baggie of pot.)

BUFF: He put up a struggle, but the forces of good won out in the end!

(Buff spies Pony.)

HEY! Pony, man! Great concert tonight!

PONY: You were there?

BUFF: No, but I heard it was great.

SOOZE: Pony, this is my friend, Bee-Bee.

PONY: Hey. How's it going?

(Everyone looks at Bee-Bee. Beat.)

BEE-BEE: Hi.

BUFF: So tell us, man! Party time. Trashing hotel rooms. Babes around the clock.

PONY: We don't have the time for that.

(Buff suddenly notices Erica sitting on the bench.)

BUFF: No? So who's this?

PONY: Erica? Erica's the publicist for the band.

BUFF: Yeah, right. "Publicist."

PONY: She works for the record company. She takes care of interviews, shit like that. Erica was backstage after the show and said she'd like to see Burnfield.

JEFF: What are we doing?

BUFF *(To Erica)***:** We're old friends of Pony's. We all go way back. To our childhood.

ERICA: He's told me. Burnfield. We all hear about Burnfield.

JEFF: What does he tell you? About how we started the band? The "early days."

ERICA: Oh, you were in the band?

JEFF: I helped start it.

PONY: Well, not exactly, Jeff.

JEFF: Yeah, for a while . . .

PONY: You came by that one day and played harmonica. But that was before we were even really a band. We were just kids fooling around.

JEFF: I came by more than once.

(Tim rouses and enters the conversation.)

TIM: Danny? Who's Danny?

SOOZE: "Danny David," their manager.

TIM: Danny David, what is that, a Jewish name? When I was in the service I knew a Jew. Pilot. Big nose. Curly hair. Always talking. Funny guy. Is Danny one of those funny kind of Jews, Pony?

PONY: I don't know.

TIM: You don't know? You don't know if he's funny or not?

ERICA: He talks a lot. He's funny.

(Tim sits next to Erica on the bench.)

TIM: So, you came by to see how the other half lives, eh? Well, here we are, what do you think? *(Pause)* Kind of like a documentary on educational TV. Isn't it?

ERICA: I think it's nice here. It's different.

TIM *(To Pony)*: What do they interview you about?

PONY: There's this benefit for Darfur we're going to do. And you know . . . my work . . .

TIM: Your "work"? What do you tell them about your "work"?

PONY: I explain what my songs are about, you know. The message: "find honesty, tear down the walls, reach out to another naked human being." How I write it, get my ideas, you know.

TIM: How *do* you get your ideas?

SOOZE: Stop it, Tim.

TIM: I want to know! I'm curious. How do you get your ideas?

SOOZE: Tim's jealous. He wants to have ideas, too.

TIM: Yeah, I'm jealous. I'm jealous of Jew-loving faggots who do benefits for starving niggers.

(Tim leans back into the bench and closes his eyes.)

SOOZE: Jeff.

JEFF: What?

(Tim's motionless. Bee-Bee smokes by herself. Pony strums his guitar. Buff has not stopped focusing on Erica.)

BUFF: You're not his publicist.

ERICA: Sure I am. It's a great job. Meet all kinds of cool people. Work on the website. Widen the demographic.

BUFF: And you're, like, what else?

ERICA: Am I his girlfriend?

BUFF: That's one way of putting it.

ERICA: Am I *fucking* him?

BUFF: Shit.

ERICA: Pony, what would you say our relationship is?

PONY: Mother-daughter.

ERICA: Pony and I are "friends."

BUFF: So like, you're available?

ERICA: In what way?

BUFF: In a horizontal and wet way.

SOOZE: Can we stop this, Buff?

TIM *(Eyes still closed)*: He's simply having verbal intercourse, Sooze.

SOOZE: No, he's not, he's objectifying her. He's entertaining us at her expense.

ERICA: It's OK. He's . . . what's your name?

BUFF: Buff.

ERICA: Buff is funny.

TIM: She likes Buff. She thinks Buff's funny. So why don't you keep your feminist hole closed?

SOOZE: Why don't you swallow your cock and choke on it? Oh, I forgot, it's too small.

TIM: Cunt . . .

JEFF: Tim . . .

TIM *(Opens his eyes; standing)*: You fucking faggot, what are you going to say?

SOOZE *(To Jeff)*: It's OK. Forget it.

TIM: Excuse me, I was speaking to the faggot.

JEFF: So Pony, where are you staying? Your mother's house?

(Tim sits back down. He closes his eyes again.)

TIM: Fucking faggot.

PONY: No, that can be kind of a hassle. I stay at the Four Seasons. It's easier.

TIM: "I STAY AT THE FOUR SEASONS. IT'S EASIER."

(Tim gets up and walks off, smiling at Erica on his way out. She smiles back.)

JEFF: The Four Seasons? Really? I hear it's nice there.

PONY: Hey, it's a bed and hot water, you know?

SOOZE: What are you doing next? I mean, what does the band do now?

PONY: Back to the studio. New album.

BUFF: Need any help? I could do the "behind the scenes" video. I make videos now, man.

PONY: You know, that would be fun. We have to do that shit all the time. You have a reel?

BUFF: Reel?

PONY: Like something I could show people?

BUFF: Sure.

PONY: Then, you never know. And I was thinking, Sooze, you should do our next cover.

SOOZE: Right. You don't want me to do your cover.

PONY: I don't want you to do the cover, I *need* you to do the cover. Did you see the last one?

SOOZE: It was pretty bad.

PONY: That's what I'm saying.

SOOZE: You're not serious.

PONY: I'm always serious.

SOOZE: They would never let me do what I want.

PONY: Actually I get final approval. It's in my contract.

SOOZE: Would I get paid?

PONY: We'd have to fly you out. For meetings.

SOOZE: Yeah?

PONY: Yeah.

SOOZE: That would be . . . that would be something I would consider doing.

PONY: Awesome!

(Pony puts down his beer, stretches and stands.)

You know something? I feel good. I feel good out with
you guys again. I forgot what it was like to just hang out.
And you know why it feels so right? Because you guys are
real, you guys have a sense of humor, you live your lives.
The guys on the road, the band, all they talk about is scor-
ing chicks. And Danny, all he thinks about is money.

BUFF: Yeah, we're above all that.

PONY: No, I mean, when we were driving out here, I told George,
the driver, to roll the windows down, just so I could smell
the air. The aroma of freshly cut grass . . . great! The hous-
es were flashing by and I could see into the picture windows. Families watching TV, eating dinner, a guy drinking
a beer. The *suburbs*! They don't call it "The American
Dream" for nothing.

(Pony receives blank stares.)

JEFF: "They." Who's "they"?

PONY: This afternoon I went by the mall and just walked around
by myself. I just wanted to be alone and get, you know,
that old mall feeling.

SOOZE: What's that?

PONY *(Strumming his guitar idly)*: You know, order, safety, security.
I've been trying to write something about it. But it's new . . .
nah . . . never mind.

BUFF: Come on, play it, man!

SOOZE: Play it!

PONY: Really? OK. Uh . . .

(Pony starts to play his guitar.)

(Buff and Sooze find a seat on the ground.)

BUFF: Free concert!!!

(Pony starts the song tentatively, then finds his voice.)

PONY:

> I get up in the morning and I go to work
> I have a car, a TV, my boss is a jerk
> My lawn's weed-free, my wife is sane
> When I wake up tomorrow, gonna do it all again . . .
>
> I drove down the highway, there was a big jam,
> A family had died inside their mini-van
> There was a back-up, you know it went for miles
> But as bad as it was, it was gone after a while.

(Chorus:)

> You may think there's nothing to it
> And the truth is hard to see
> To be a man invisible
> Is a remarkable thing to be.
> Thing to be . . . Thing to be . . . Thing to be.

ERICA: Nice! That's a keeper!
BUFF: I'm glad you put "TV" in your song, man. That's important.
BEE-BEE: I like the part about the "man invisible."
SOOZE: Oh, yeah, really. And your singing's gotten so good.
PONY: I take lessons.
SOOZE: Really.
JEFF: So, the "man invisible" is . . . who? I don't get it.

(Pony addresses Sooze in answer to Jeff:)

PONY: Like "everyman," like *Homo americanus.*

JEFF: No, I mean, if we're like the "man invisible," that includes you?

PONY: Well, no, I'm . . . an artist. You know, there's life, and then there's the artist watching the life, commenting on it.

JEFF: Everyone does that.

PONY: What?

JEFF: Comment. Say things. Think. Whatever. Why are you so special?

PONY: Well, it's one thing to think. It's another thing to communicate it to people. I'm doing that with my music. "If a tree falls in the forest and no one's there to hear it, does it make a sound?"

JEFF: Of course it does!

SOOZE: That's my worst fear. Making a sound and no one hears it.

PONY: Mine, too.

BUFF: Wait. What happened to the tree?

JEFF: Hold on a second!

PONY: You know what I'm saying?

SOOZE: Sure, you make art, you want people to see it.

JEFF: Yeah, sure. But that doesn't mean your tree is not artistic if no one cuts it down.

SOOZE: Jeff likes to argue for the sake of arguing.

JEFF: No, I don't.

SOOZE: Yes, you do.

JEFF: I don't.

SOOZE: You do.

JEFF *(Walking away):* No. I don't.

(Buff focuses on Erica.)

BUFF: You come from, like, a town like this?

ERICA: Sort of. I come from an "area."

(Tim reenters sipping a king-size beer, a fresh six-pack under his arm. He sits, finishes his beer, tosses it, then pops open a new can.)

BUFF: Oh. Cool. Not "South Central"?

ERICA: No. Not South Central.

TIM: What "area"?

ERICA: Hmmmmm?

TIM: Not South Central. Where?

ERICA: Bel-Air.

(Beat.)

TIM: You rich?

ERICA: Not really. Middle class.

TIM: Me, too. Middle class.

ERICA: Maybe upper-middle class.

TIM: Yeah. So your dad's a big deal, huh?

ERICA: He thinks so. No, he is.

(Erica has found herself surrounded by the group. Tim approaches her.)

TIM: You love him a lot, he bought you a BMW for your birthday, but finally you had to move out and get your own place. *(He holds a hand over her head and shuts his eyes, speaking like a mind reader)* Your parents hate your smoking. You didn't tell them about the abortion, did you? You know your dad's having an affair with someone at work. You used to be bulimic, but now you're over it. You subscribe to *Vanity Fair*. You've been seeing the same therapist for years. You have your nails done by a professional. You love yoga.

BUFF *(To Jeff)*: What's he doing, man?

TIM *(Continuing his analysis)*: You go to a private high school?

ERICA: Yes. I know you despise everything I stand for.

TIM: I never said that. I just like to know who I'm dealing with.

ERICA: Now you know. What are you going to do about it?

TIM: Hey, Neil, what was that song you played at the prom? Wasn't it "I Believe I Can Fly"?

JEFF: No, man, it was "Wind Beneath My Wings."

TIM: Oh, that's right. That's right. *(Claps his hands)*

SOOZE *(To Pony)*: I bought your CD.

PONY: You did?

SOOZE: I like that one, "Salvation."

PONY: Really?

SOOZE *(Firmly)*: Play it?

PONY: I dunno, I should get going. I have to get up pretty early tomorrow morning.

ERICA: You have the "eight A.M." call.

SOOZE: Please?

PONY: Yeah?

(Sooze nods.)

OK.

(Unnoticed, Bee-Bee gets up and exists, taking the boombox with her.
Pony serenades Sooze.)

I know it's not easy to open your eyes
See what's around you, listen to their lies
They are old, we are young
They are fat, we are fun
They're asleep, we are new
They will die, I love you.

I feel like an idiot watching the parade
I know there's no tomorrow, only the charade

> I am dead deep inside
> In my head, all the lies
> There's no then, only now
> I will love, show me how.

(Chorus:)

> I burnt my hand in a fire
> Haven't slept for a week
> Cut my feet on the glass
> Never finding what I seek
> I need salvation . . . I need salvation . . . I need salva-
>   tion . . .
> Kiss my wounds.

(Sooze and Pony are in their own world. Jeff suddenly kicks the trash can over and stands.)

JEFF: Hey! Pony!

PONY: Huh?

JEFF: If we wanted to hear you sing, we would have gone to your concert.

SOOZE: What a nice thing to say, Jeff.

JEFF: You ride in here like fucking God! You're a big deal! You've been everywhere, you know everything. Fuck you!

PONY: I didn't say I know everything.

JEFF: Well, you don't.

(Jeff kicks the trash can again.)

SOOZE: Jeff!

JEFF: So you sold ninety thousand units. So what? Is that supposed to mean you're a genius, an artist? You're higher up the ladder? You got an extra gold star on your forehead?

TIM: Jeff, you're cute when you're angry.

JEFF: Why don't you write a song about having dinner with Johnny Depp?

PONY: What are you saying, Jeff? You don't like my stuff, I won't sing it. Sorry.

JEFF: That's not it. I'm saying . . . I'm saying . . . I don't need a limo to know who I am. OK? I don't need a website.

TIM: OK! Right on!

JEFF *(Quietly)*: I know that I *don't* know. I know that much. I know that things are fucked-up beyond belief and I know I have nothing original to say about any of it. I don't have an answer, I don't have a "message."

TIM: He isn't crying, is he?

JEFF: Shut up, Tim, it's not funny!

TIM: But it is!

PONY: Jeff, now listen . . .

(Jeff swings wildly at Pony, and ends up falling down. Pause. He sits up.)

BUFF *(Cheery)*: Hey, man, chill! *(Hands Jeff a beer)*

JEFF: "Man invisible."

PONY: Hey, man, I'm sorry if I said something wrong.

JEFF: It's OK. It's not you. It's this sidewalk. This cell. This void. You know?

PONY: No, look, I come here, and I'm so used to everyone kissing my ass I think I'm a fucking star, and I'm sorry if I'm full of attitude. *(Puts his arm around Jeff)*

JEFF: It's not you. It's not anybody. It's me.

PONY: Hey, man, it's OK!

JEFF: I have no brain. No eyes. The blind leading the blind. FUCK!

PONY: No, look, uh. Why don't we get something to eat? George can drive us, there's plenty of room in the stretch.

(Pony glances at Sooze as he massages Jeff's shoulders.)

SOOZE: Chinese. Hung Suk takeout is open till one.

JEFF: Go pick something up and bring it back here.

PONY: Sure. But come with us, man. I said I would give you a ride in the limo. You, too, Buff! Tim!

BUFF: Wicked!

TIM: I'm allergic to limos.

(Sooze comes over to Jeff and holds his lapels.)

SOOZE: Come on.

JEFF: Go ahead.

SOOZE: I'm not going if you don't come.

BUFF *(To Jeff)*: Come on, man. You can hang me out the window! I'll do tricks. I'll puke on people for you.

(Jeff smiles at this.)

JEFF: I don't feel like it. That's all.

SOOZE: Why don't you just try? Where's Bee-Bee?

(Jeff stands. They all start walking, except Erica, who lags behind. Sooze and Jeff exit.)

PONY: You coming, Erica?

ERICA: No, I have to catch up with my calls.

SOOZE *(From offstage)*: Bee-Bee! Where'd you go?

(Pony "reads" Erica. She wants to stay behind.)

PONY: OK. *(He goes)*

(Buff watches Erica.)

BUFF: You sure?

(Erica preoccupies herself, stubbing out a cigarette, pretending not to hear him.)

JEFF *(From offstage)*: BUFF!

(Buff exits. Erica lights another cigarette. She moves toward Tim. Tim drinks.)

ERICA: Well, you got everything right but the car. My dad didn't get me a BMW, it was a Porsche.

(Beat.)

You seem to know a lot about me. I don't know anything about you. What kind of music do you like?

TIM: Military marching bands. *(Finishes his beer and throws the can. He opens another)*

ERICA: You know where Bel-Air is, don't you? You know what it is.

TIM: I saw it once on TV.

ERICA: You think I'm rich and you hate me.

TIM: Don't tell me what I think. You don't know me.

ERICA: If I don't, I want to.

TIM: No, you don't.

ERICA: You were in the army?

(Tim drinks.)

TIM: Navy. Air Support. Stationed in Diego García. Middle of fucking nowhere. Biggest mistake of my life.

ERICA: Air Support? You were a pilot?

TIM: Oh yeah, me and Tom Cruise.

Signed up to be a Navy flyer. Gonna go fight for Operation Iraqi Freedom. What did I know about officer training school or having a college degree or coming from the right family?

ERICA: I don't understand.

TIM: They didn't need pilots, they needed slaves. So I spent all day packing munitions into B-1s and B-52s. Every night drinking tax-free booze, and the rest of the time kissing officer ass. Never saw one day of action.

ERICA: Why aren't you still there?

TIM: There was a bar fight. I didn't start it. I didn't even hurt anybody.

ERICA: So you never got to Iraq?

TIM: Fuck Iraq.

(Tim drinks. Erica says nothing. Silence.)

I got wounded though. *(Tim stands. He puts his pinky finger in the air)* Crushed my little finger under an engine mount. *(Erica grabs his hand and holds it)* So they gave me an honorable discharge to get rid of my ass. Disabled while serving. I get a check every month. *(Uncomfortable, he takes his hand back)*

ERICA: I guess you get some kind of experience from it.

TIM: Oh yeah. I'm much smarter now. I got taught a big lesson: shut up and stay where you belong. Learn your place or lose your place.

ERICA: And not so happy?

(Tim smiles weakly at her.)

TIM: Happy? That's your game. I pass.

ERICA: Who said I'm happy? A day in the life: go to the office, return calls, salad for lunch, go to the gym, check the voice-mail, more calls, punch the Blackberry, smoke the low-tar cigarette, practice my yoga, shop for shoes.

Most of the time I don't feel anything, just a mild anticipation, like, "Maybe some big star will visit backstage after the show tonight." "Maybe there'll be a party somewhere." I guess I'm hoping for the unexpected. *(She tries to meet Tim's eyes)* You know, Pony told me about his friends in Burnfield, but frankly from what he said I figured you were just a bunch of kids. I really came out here for the pizza. He told me it was incredible.

TIM: It is.

ERICA: No, but I mean underneath all the noise, you're not like the rest of them. You're a serious guy. Aren't you? Wise in a way. Interesting.

TIM: What was you name?

ERICA: Erica.

TIM: You think you and I are alike, Erica?

ERICA: Deep down. Way down. I think we're both looking for more. You know?

TIM: It's a mistake to think that.

ERICA: We can still talk. It's nice to talk.

TIM: It's "nice" to do a lot of things.

ERICA: That's what I mean.

TIM: You don't understand what I'm saying here.

ERICA: I want to understand.

TIM: I'm not a "serious guy." I'm not "interesting."

ERICA: Then what are you?

TIM: Harmful to others.

ERICA: Hey, I'm a big girl. If I didn't want to be here, I'd be in a limo right now with a bunch of kids. Cruising for Chinese food.

TIM: You don't know.

ERICA: No?

TIM: No.

(Erica steps right up to him.)

ERICA: So teach me a lesson.

(Tim kisses her fiercely. Erica returns the aggression. She reaches for his crotch, rubs him. Tim breaks away.)

TIM: Whoaaa . . . You sure about this?

(Erica nods yes. Tim leads her off.)

Act Three

The storefront is shuttered.

Bee-Bee sits, her back against the wall, smoking a cigarette, Buff's boombox next to her. Music plays. An unopened quart bottle of Jack Daniels sits before her. She watches the bottle as if it were about to speak to her.

Tim is curled up asleep on the ground, at the other end of the wall.

Jeff enters. He sees Bee-Bee and the bottle, notes Tim sleeping, then snaps off the radio.

JEFF: I just walked all the way from the center to here.

(Bee-Bee doesn't answer.)

I haven't walked that far since Junior High.

(Beat.)

You know you missed the big limo ride. We were looking for you.

BEE-BEE: How was it?

JEFF: Disgusting. And stupid. I got out. *(Nudging Tim with his foot)* Tim! Get up!

(Tim doesn't stir. Jeff notices the bottle of booze.)

I thought you didn't drink.

BEE-BEE: I don't. Anymore.

JEFF: Uh-huh. Can I have some?

BEE-BEE: Knock yourself out.

(Jeff takes the bottle, uncaps it, and takes a swig.)

JEFF: Tim! *(Motionless, Tim could be dead. He takes another swig)* It's weird how things can change. One minute everything is fucked, and, then, you look at it from a different angle and it all makes sense. I walked for twenty minutes and everything suddenly became clear. You know? People used to walk a lot more than they do now, and I don't think they worried about things half as much as we do.

BEE-BEE: Yeah?

JEFF: Ever hear the saying: "This too shall pass"?

BEE-BEE: Sure, all the time. In group.

JEFF: "Group"?

BEE-BEE: Rehab. Outpatient. I have to go once a week. It's kind a like AA.

JEFF: Oh yeah, you had to go to Highgate. You stole a car or something.

BEE-BEE: Or something.

JEFF: How long were you in there?

BEE-BEE: Ninety days. But now I just go once a week. I'm rehabilitated, see?

(Jeff swigs from the bottle.)

JEFF: You shouldn't drink, then. Are you gonna drink?

BEE-BEE: No. Yes. Maybe. Fuck.

JEFF: That would suck if you had to go back . . . to rehab.

BEE-BEE: It would suck big time. I'd kill myself first.

JEFF: Is it really bad?

BEE-BEE: It was hell with windows. So noisy, I always had a head-
ache. Smelly. Shit on the walls. There were kids my age
sucking their thumbs, wetting their pants. Most of us were
there because of drugs, but you wanna know something
funny? There were more drugs inside that fucking place
than I ever saw on the outside. A kid from my floor shot
up cough medicine, had convulsions right in front of me.

JEFF: Fuck.

BEE-BEE: Every day I woke up in my "cell" and I thought to myself,
My parents put me here. Why? Because I stayed out all
night one time. Because I broke the VCR when I was
drunk. Because I was "out of control." I thought my parents loved me.

JEFF: They were trying to help.

BEE-BEE: Yeah. That's one way of looking at it.

JEFF: So now you don't drink?

BEE-BEE: I'm rehabilitated. I'm a productive member of society.
I can *deal*—"one day at a fucking time."

JEFF: You're pissed off at Buff. But Buff's a riot. He can be funny as
shit.

BEE-BEE: Yeah?

JEFF: Sex is a weird thing. I mean when you think about it, we're
just like these organisms with bizarre tentacles and ori-
fices kind of poking and pushing into each other. Doing
these insane courtship dances. Getting all emotional
about biology.

BEE-BEE: I don't know.

(Jeff absentmindedly drinks the whiskey.)

JEFF: I was pretty down before too. But we were riding around and everyone's getting all excited and suddenly it just hit me what we were doing. We're getting off on the fact that we're in a car five feet longer than the rest. I got out and just started walking.

BEE-BEE: Good.

JEFF: No, see, what it was—I didn't want to admit it, but I was jealous of Pony.

BEE-BEE: Sure. He's rich and famous. He's got everything and you've got nothing.

JEFF: But I mean, when I was walking, I realized: he's stuck in that limo all the time, he's stuck with the autographs and the interviews. He has to do what his manager tells him to do. He isn't free. He's just part of the machine. And freedom's really all there is.

BEE-BEE: Freedom.

JEFF: It used to scare me that I didn't know what was coming in my life. I always thought, What if I make the wrong move? You know? But maybe there isn't any right move. I was trying to figure it all out. But maybe you can't.

(Bee-Bee doesn't answer. Jeff stands up, slightly drunk.)

Look at us. We all dress the same, we all talk the same, we all watch the same TV. No one's really different, even if they think they're different. "Oh boy, look at my tattoo!" You know?

(Bee-Bee is barely paying attention. Jeff is oblivious.)

And that makes me free, because I can do anything if I really don't care what the result is. I don't need money. I don't even need a future. I could knock out all my teeth with a hammer, so what? I could poke my eyes out. I'd still be alive. Strip naked and fart in the wind. At least I would know I was doing something real for two or three seconds. It's all about fear. And I'm not afraid anymore. Fuck it!

(Jeff begins to strip. Bee-Bee watches him flatly. Then, as if in a daze, she takes the bottle and drinks.)

Because anything is possible. It is night on the planet Earth, and I am alive, and some day I will be dead. Some day, I'll be bones in a box. But right now, I'm not. And anything is possible. And that's why I can go to New York with Sooze. Because each moment can be what it is. I'm on the train going there, I'm living there, I'm reading a newspaper, I'm walking down the street. There is no failure, there is no mistake. I just go and live there and what happens, happens.

(Jeff is down to his underwear.)

So at this moment, I am getting naked. And I am not afraid. FUCK FEAR! FUCK MONEY! I WILL GO TO NEW YORK AND I WILL LIVE IN A BOX. I WILL SING WITH THE BUMS. I WILL STARVE, BUT I WILL NOT DIE. I WILL LIVE. I WILL TALK TO GOD!

(Jeff and Bee-Bee haven't noticed Nazeer standing in the shadows. Jeff starts to pull off his underwear. Then he sees Nazeer and stops dead in his tracks. Instinctively, he reaches for his pants.)

NAZEER: Don't you guys ever go home?
JEFF: What's your fucking problem?
NAZEER: What's yours?
JEFF: You fucking scared me, man!

NAZEER: My sister wanted me to check the store. She's afraid you and your friends are going to break the windows.

JEFF: That's stupid.

NAZEER: You're standing in the middle of the street with your penis sticking out and you're calling my sister stupid?

(Jeff grabs more clothes and starts to dress.)

JEFF: Tim, look who's here. Hadji.

(Jeff again nudges Tim with his foot, gets no reaction. He continues to dress. Nazeer walks around them, checking out the mess they've made, as well as Tim lying on the ground. He starts cleaning up. Through all of this, Bee-Bee sits motionless, smoking, looking at the ground.)

NAZEER: We had a servant in Karachi who took to drinking. She died a beggar.

JEFF: Just because I'm having a couple of shots of Jack Daniels doesn't mean I'm an alcoholic.

NAZEER: Uh-huh.

JEFF: Besides, how could you have had a servant? I thought you were poor.

NAZEER: We were *not* poor. In fact, some cousins of mine are very wealthy. And also, in fact, at one point we had a cook, a gardener, and I had a personal tutor. How do you think I learned to speak English so well? Or do you ever think about anything?

JEFF: So why did you come here, if you had it so fucking great?

NAZEER: One of my wealthy cousins spoke out when the military took over. He was arrested in the middle of the night. We have not seen him since. Our circle of friends, students, professors at the university, artists, were frightened by the new regime. I thought it made sense to leave the country.

JEFF: "Artists"?

NAZEER: Yes, "artists." My sister is a dancer. She was hoping to attend the National Academy. But we left. Instead.

JEFF: Uh-huh.

NAZEER: For a while we had a shop in Southall. That's in London . . . England?

JEFF: I know where London is.

NAZEER: The Islamic radicals making speeches in the park made life more difficult for me, for my sister. Violent people, nobody likes them. Anyway, our main problem was the blacks. They would come in stealing things. I would argue with them. Then one night they burnt our shop to the ground. For some reason I thought it would be different here.

JEFF: We're not like those people.

(Nazeer stops picking up.)

NAZEER *(Very direct):* Let me give you some advice. You seem like a smart guy. This is not for you. This, what you are doing with your life. You know?

JEFF *(Walking away from Nazeer):* Thanks for the advice, but you wouldn't understand what's going on with me.

NAZEER: Very complicated.

JEFF: That's right.

NAZEER: Complicated or not, life moves on, eh?

(Looking at Bee-Bee, sitting off by herself) Is she all right?

JEFF: Everyone's fine. We're all fine.

NAZEER: Well, if you're all so fine, why don't you all go home? And take him with you, otherwise, I might sweep him up in the morning with the trash.

(Nazeer exits.

Jeff and Bee-Bee say nothing for a few seconds. Jeff nudges Tim again.)

JEFF: Tim!

(Beat.)

BEE-BEE: Jeff?

JEFF: Yeah?

BEE-BEE: Nothin'.

JEFF: What?

BEE-BEE: Do you . . . do you ever get up in the morning and think, Well, here's another day, just like the last one? *(Pause)* You know? Like what difference does it make? The days just keep coming, one after another . . . so—

JEFF: I think that sometimes.

BEE-BEE: But I mean, if you lived them or not, what difference would it make, you know?

(Sooze and Pony enter carrying bags of Chinese food and two six-packs.)

JEFF: Food! I thought you guys got lost.

SOOZE: We took the scenic route past the high school. You would have enjoyed it.

(Jeff picks up a carton of fried rice. Pony takes out food and eats. Jeff moves toward Tim again.)

JEFF: Tim, come on!

SOOZE *(To Bee-Bee)*: Where did you go?

BEE-BEE: Home.

JEFF *(To Tim)*: Get up.

SOOZE: Something wrong?

BEE-BEE: Nah . . . you know.

SOOZE: Get your exercise, Jeff?

JEFF: I just got sick of listening to that demo tape over and over. I felt like a groupie.

SOOZE: I enjoyed the ride. I'm sorry you didn't.

JEFF: Wait a second . . . I don't want to fight. Listen, I'm sorry . . .

SOOZE: What?!

JEFF: I'm sorry. I mean it. When I got out of the limo I walked all the way from the center to here and I figured something out.

SOOZE: Oh yeah?

BUFF *(From offstage, shout-singing a drunken lyric)*: "JUMP AROUND . . . JUMP AROUND . . ."

(Buff comes bounding in, getting in Jeff's face.)

"JUMP, JUMP, JUMP AROUND!"

(Buff bounces through the group and falls down.)

SOOZE: He threw up out the window of the limo.

(Through all of this, Tim has gotten up, surreptitiously steals the Jack Daniels, and hoists himself up onto the roof.
Buff gets up, brushes himself off, and goes for the food. He scoops up a pint of fried rice and eats with relish.)

BUFF: When I'm shit-faced, I get this huge appetite. I love to eat. Don't know why. Most people don't, but I do.

(All watch with amazement as Buff sucks down the entire pint of rice.)

Oh shit!

(Buff starts puking his guts out. He finishes. Pause. He rolls onto his back, groaning.)

Oh, wow, I don't feel good.

SOOZE: He should go home.

PONY: I don't think George'll let him into the limo like that. He already had to clean down the side.

JEFF: I'll take him.

SOOZE: You sure?

BUFF: Ohhhhhh!

(Jeff helps Buff to his feet.)

JEFF *(To Sooze):* Come with me! I want to tell you something!

SOOZE: I'm hungry . . . I didn't eat at my sister's.

JEFF: Never mind, I'll be right back.

BUFF: Shit. I probably shouldn't have done that.

(Jeff exits with Buff.
Sooze picks up some food. Pony starts laughing.)

PONY: Burnfield! There's no place like it.

SOOZE: Burnfield—"Pizza and Puke Capitol of the World."

PONY: I can't believe you're still here.

SOOZE: I'm moving to New York.

PONY: If . . .

SOOZE: No, I'm going. Soon.

PONY: Uh-huh.

SOOZE: What's that supposed to mean?

PONY: I say what I mean.

SOOZE: You think you're so smart.

PONY: That's because I am.

(Sooze walks toward the back of the store, facing into the dark-
ness, "the woods.")

SOOZE: See how it gets dark down there, through those little trees and shit. What do you think is down there?

PONY: Old tires? Bottles?

SOOZE: When I was a little girl, all those condos over there were woods. And a big stream ran down there into a little pond. There were ducks.

PONY: Where's the stream now?

SOOZE: Who knows? It's probably drained into a pipe underground, we just can't see it. They filled in the pond.

(Pony grabs his food and hauls himself up onto the dumpster.)

I had a brother who was, you know, retarded? Down's syndrome. Mikey was always eating because he wasn't that good at *doing* things? He could walk places by himself, that was it. It was safe to let him do that in those days. So he used to walk over here in the afternoon, and this lady who worked in the bakery would give him a doughnut, and he would sit on the steps and eat the doughnut. I think the lady used to talk to him. And he liked that. Mikey was getting pretty fat from all the doughnuts and shit, but you figure, let him have his fun, you know? That winter it got wicked cold, and that same year the bakery closed. No more nice lady. No more doughnuts. But Mikey'd still come down here, looking for the doughnut lady. And one day, Mikey didn't come home when he was supposed to. *(Pause)* We didn't find him until the spring when the ice melted. They figured he had fallen through the ice on the pond. Then he got sucked under, down the stream. He had been pushed under the ice all the way down the stream to a place where there was an old shopping cart some kids had tossed in. *(Pause)* And there he was underwater in the rusty old cart, still wearing his overalls, all decayed. But it was him.

PONY: You found him?

SOOZE: No. Some kids. But I saw him.

PONY: Your own brother.

SOOZE *(Moves back to him, leaving the "woods")*: It was ten years ago. I'm over it. My mother's not, she blames herself. All she does is watch the Home Shopping Network and drink. I keep telling her to go to therapy, you know? My Dad, I never see my Dad. Vietnam vet. I think he killed people over there. I used to wonder if Mikey was like his bad karma come back to get us. Anyway, he lives in Florida, skippers deep-sea fishing parties. *(Pause)* I hate it here. It's ugly. It's like being dead. You went away. I want to go away.

PONY *(Jumping off the dumpster)*: Yeah, "away." It's not always so great either. I mean, I don't want to come back, but I get homesick, sometimes.

SOOZE: Yeah? That's hard to imagine.

PONY: No, it can be really frustrating. Tonight I had to do this interview and the things they ask are so stupid. But I do it, because the work's important, you know? I do it for the work. I have to protect the work.

SOOZE: But it's gotta be gratifying.

PONY: Sure. And it's hard. Every night a new city. Pressure from my manager and my lawyer to write new stuff. I'll write a beautiful song and they're like: "But what will the video look like?"

SOOZE: Or the album cover.

PONY: Or the album cover. *(Smiles at her)* Sometimes I try to remember why I left in the first place. I think about people. I wonder what they're doing. I thought about you. A lot.

SOOZE: Me?

PONY: I did.

SOOZE: Yeah, when you called, I thought, *there's* a name from the past.

PONY: Or a name from the future.

(Beat.)

I mean, we'll be working on the cover, right?

(Voices are heard from offstage.)

SOOZE: I know what you're getting at.

PONY: You do?

SOOZE: I like you, too, Pony. *(Takes his hand)* My mother has a saying: "Don't write any checks you can't cash."

PONY: Sooze . . .

(Jeff enters.)

JEFF: He won't let me take him home.

(Buff enters, carrying a plaster lawn gnome. He presents it to Pony.)

BUFF: On behalf of Burnfield: I present you with the keys to the city!

(Tim climbs down off the roof. He calmly walks over to the food and picks through it.)

TIM: What's to eat? I'm starving.

(Buff grabs a beer and pops it.)

BUFF: Gotta settle my stomach.

TIM: How was the limo ride? Thrilling?

SOOZE: It was the nicest thing I've done in a long time.

TIM. Good. Very good.

PONY: Where's Erica?

(Tim picks out a rib, sits, and eats it.)

TIM: Erica? She said she was feeling tired. Went back to the hotel.

PONY: Oh. *(Puzzled)* How did she get back?

TIM: I called Bucky's and got her a cab.

PONY: Oh.

TIM: Did they give you hot mustard?

PONY: I gotta go out to the car for a sec. I'll be right back. *(Exits to the limo)*

BUFF *(Shouting into Tim's ear)*: "JUMP AROUND!"

(Tim takes a swipe at Buff.)

TIM: Fuck off!

(Jeff approaches Sooze.)

JEFF: I have to talk to you. There's something I figured out.

SOOZE: You smell like whiskey.

JEFF: No. Listen. We have to talk.

SOOZE: Is that a threat?

TIM: I ate a dog in Thailand. It tasted a lot like this sparerib.

JEFF: I thought about New York.

SOOZE: Forget New York. I don't want to talk about New York anymore.

TIM: There was a restaurant where they served live monkey brains. I tried to get in, but I didn't have any money with me. And my mother has a saying: "Don't write any checks you can't cash."

JEFF: Tim, what the fuck you talking about?

TIM: Ask your girlfriend.

(Pony reenters.)

PONY: I called Erica's cell. No answer.

TIM: What are you, her dad? She said she might go for a drink first.

PONY: She always answers her phone.

TIM: She's a big girl. She's all right.

PONY: What did she say?

TIM: About what?

PONY: About where she went. What bar?

TIM: I don't know. The bar at the hotel.

PONY: The bar at the hotel. She told you this? What exactly did she tell you?

TIM: Well, *Dad*, she told me she wanted to suck my cock.

PONY: Oh. Uh-huh.

TIM: She told me you wanted to suck my cock, too.

(Pony and Sooze exchange glances.)

PONY: I think I gotta go.

TIM: Don't go! Aren't you going to suck my cock?

PONY *(To Sooze)*: I'm gonna go back to the hotel and make sure she's all right.

TIM: She's fine. Don't you believe me?

PONY: I think you're a sick fuck.

TIM: Blow me.

PONY: Fuck you, I never did anything to you.

(Tim throws his rib to the ground and leaps to his feet.)

TIM: Watch your language, chief, or I might have to.

(Pony picks up his guitar and turns to go. Tim rushes after him. He drunkenly puts his arm around him.)

Wait, wait, wait! I'm sorry. I was just screwing with you, man! You rock stars are so sensitive!

SOOZE *(To Pony)*: Uh, Pony, mind if I come along?

TIM: What a great idea!

SOOZE: Just going for a ride!

TIM: No, no, that's it! Give her a ride! That would be nice! You could give her a nice ride in the backseat all the way back to the hotel.

BUFF: In the limo!

SOOZE: Tim, go throw up somewhere.

PONY: You know what? It's none of your business what I do.

TIM: None of my business? You're fucking my best friend's girl-friend and it's none of my business?

SOOZE: What the fuck are you talking about?

PONY: Nobody's fucking anybody.

TIM: You're fucking with *me*. You're fucking with my best friend.

(Tim steps into Pony. Beat.)

PONY *(Even)*: You hit me, my lawyer will drop a felony assault charge on you faster than you can say AA. You think the air force sucked, wait till you get a taste of prison.

(Pony walks away from Tim. Jeff moves in on Sooze.)

JEFF: Wait a minute. What are you doing, Sooze?

SOOZE: I'm leaving with Pony. Is that all right with you? Do I have your permission? Or maybe you have to "think" about it.

JEFF: Where are you going?

SOOZE: For a ride!

JEFF: Away?

SOOZE: Yeah, *away*. Away. Away. Away!!!

JEFF: To his hotel?

SOOZE: Shit, Jeff!

JEFF: So you can do an album cover?

SOOZE: Jeff, I've run out of words.

JEFF: Are you telling me something?

SOOZE: I don't know. And I don't care that I don't know.

JEFF: So, what about us?

SOOZE: What about us? I'm moving away, you're staying here.

JEFF: Maybe.

SOOZE: Oh, so now it's "maybe." You think I'm with somebody else so now it's "maybe."

JEFF: No!

SOOZE: Wow. Wow. You're unbelievable.

JEFF: I was thinking . . . I figured something out.

SOOZE: I bet you did.

JEFF: Hey, you know what? Do what you want! Go with him.

PONY: Hey, man. We're just going for a ride.

BUFF: In the limo!

JEFF: Oh yeah?

PONY: Yeah. That's all.

TIM: What's your lawyer's number? Gimme his number, I'll call him right now!

(Pony grabs Sooze's hand. Buff moves to exit with them.)

PONY: Sooze. I gotta go. Are you coming? Or staying?

SOOZE: Bye Jeff.

JEFF: Just go!

SOOZE: What?

JEFF: Just go.

SOUZE: You really suck, you know that?

JEFF: Go.

(Pony, Sooze and Buff leave.
Jeff joins Tim.
In the course of last this scene, Bee-Bee has become virtually a part of the woodwork, hidden in shadows.
Tim brings out the purloined bottle of Jack Daniels.)

TIM: A toast to womanhood.

(Tim drinks, then passes the bottle to Jeff. Jeff takes a long swig.)

Without suffering, Jeff, you will never have knowledge.

JEFF: I'm not suffering, because I'm not jealous of Pony.

TIM: No?

JEFF: No, man. I don't want her, not who she is now.

TIM: As long as you really believe it. As long as you're not a coward.

JEFF: I can't think.

TIM: You say "think," you're talking about "fear." It's like a black rubber bag over your head. All your philosophy. Just there to cover the obvious.

JEFF: No. I understand something now. It's no big deal.

TIM: No, it's no big deal. He's got her right where he wants her. In the back of his limo. Talking about his tour, about his "ideas." She's looking up at him with her big brown eyes.

JEFF: No.

TIM: In about twenty minutes they'll be in his suite. They'll talk for a while. Maybe they'll talk for hours. About life, about their "work." They'll feel close and warm with each other. She'll start to trust him. They'll decide to sleep with each other but not "do anything." By six A.M., they'll be making the beast with two backs. It's human nature, Jeff. She can't help herself and he can't help himself. That's the way it is, man. So go home, jerk off, pass out, and you will have completed your mission on this earth for one more day.

(Beat. Jeff has no answer.)

There's really only one answer.

JEFF: What?

TIM: Fuck 'em.

JEFF: Fuck 'em.

TIM: No man, like this: FUCK 'EM!!!

(Tim whips a carton of rice at the store.)

JEFF: Fuck 'em all!

(Jeff throws a carton of food at the store.)

Fuck 'em all!

TIM: Now you're getting it. Now you're learning. *(Pause)* Hey, I'm going home. I have a hard day of drinking tomorrow. *(Begins to exit)*

JEFF: Tim? Wait . . .

(Tim stops.)

What happened before with that Erica chick?

TIM: Nothing.

JEFF: Why'd she leave?

TIM: She came on to me. I wasn't . . . interested.

JEFF: Oh. *(Pause)* She came on to you?

TIM: Yeah, I mean, I fucked around with her a little, but . . .

JEFF: She didn't want to—

TIM: Oh she wanted to . . . but . . . you know . . . I had her around back in the van, and it's going hot and heavy. She's this animal, right?

JEFF: Yeah?

TIM: And I looked down at her and suddenly, uh, I wasn't into it.

JEFF: Why?

TIM: Why? Because . . . because I know who she is. I know what she is. I knew what she wanted. A souvenir from Burnfield. Well, I wasn't going to give it to her. Fucking bitch.

JEFF: You told her to get lost?

TIM: I did more than that.

JEFF: What did you do? Why did she leave Tim?

(Tim doesn't answer.)

TIM: I was drunk, I don't know what happened. I just got angry.

JEFF: You didn't hit her? . . .

(Long beat. Tim finally meets Jeff's eyes.)

TIM: I don't think I hit her. I don't know what happened. I gotta go.

JEFF: You don't know? How many times did you hit her?

TIM: I gotta go.

JEFF: Where is she now?

TIM: I dunno. I left her in the van.

(Jeff is frozen. He looks at Tim.)

JEFF: In the van?

(Tim doesn't answer.)

What happened, Tim?

(Tim doesn't answer.)

Tim? We . . . have to . . .

TIM: Fuck *her*! I'm going home. You should, too. What's done is done. For both of us.

(Tim moves to go again.)

JEFF: But . . .

TIM *(Putting his arm around Jeff)*: It's the way it is, pal, it's the way it is.

(Tim leaves.

Jeff moves toward the back of the store, the van, then stops. He's stuck. He views the mess lying all around him, then half-heartedly starts to pick up the Chinese food containers and throw them in the garbage can. Suddenly he stops. He heads to the van.

Bee-Bee moves out of the shadows. She picks up the bottle of Jack Daniels and swigs it. Then she takes out a vial of pills. She opens the vial, takes out a handful of pills, and lines ten of them on the curb. She pulls out her cell phone and dials. She pops a pill, then swigs the booze.)

BEE-BEE: Hey, it's me. Just wanted to check in. Listen, um, don't worry about me, I just wasn't up for the hotel thing. And, uh, I'm home. And, um, so, uh, OK. *(Puts another pill in her mouth and swigs)* But listen, Sooze? Sooze? I just wanted to tell you, I thought the piece went really great tonight. And I had some ideas and I emailed them to you. Like maybe instead of one projector, you get three projectors . . . and also I was thinking about atom-bomb mushroom clouds? I know it's kind of a cliché, but like the apocalypse is the ultimate male fantasy. *(Pill, swig. Her phone beeps)* Oh shit. So anyway, gotta have that. And more stuff about sex. And sperm. I think. And also maybe the space shuttle. Fuck! my batteries are dying. Uh, I should go. But have a good time, OK? And be careful. And I love you. *(Her phone battery dies)* Fuck. *(She smiles, then takes a swig)*

(Blackout.)

Act Four

Morning. The store is open for business.

Nazeer is picking up the mess left by the group outside the store. Pakeesa is working the counter.

Nazeer doesn't notice Jeff, sitting around the corner behind the store.

Buff enters, bounces past Nazeer and into the store, buys a package of Devil Dogs and comes out of the store, eating. He watches Nazeer work.

BUFF: Beautiful fucking day, man.

(Buff finishes the Devil Dogs. He drops the crumpled package on the ground. Then, before Nazeer can react, Buff scoops up his trash.)

Sorry, chief.

(Buff takes a standing jump shot at the trash can.)

Swish!

(He makes the shot, then turns to go.)

NAZEER: That's OK for you. That's OK. Enjoy yourself.

BUFF: You talking to me?

NAZEER: That's OK.

BUFF: Good, I'm glad it's OK.

NAZEER: When I get my engineering degree and I'm swimming in my swimming pool, it will be very fucking OK.

BUFF: Hey, if you're talking to me, make some sense. I don't speak Swahili.

NAZEER: In two more years, I will have an engineering degree. We will sell the store. We will move away from Burnfield and the store and you standing here.

BUFF: Good. See you later. *(Moves to leave)*

NAZEER: You are a drunk and a bum.

(Buff stops.)

BUFF: Your sister sucks my cock every night, swallows my come and loves it.

NAZEER: That's OK. We have a saying back where I come from: "Either the salt is rotten or the meat."

BUFF: You're not so smart, chief. I'm moving out to L.A.

NAZEER: That's nice. They have many 7-Elevens there for you to stand in front of.

(Nazeer enters the store.
  Buff discovers Jeff behind the store.)

BUFF: Hey, man.

JEFF: Hey.

BUFF: Whoa, you look like shit. Didn't you go home last night?
JEFF: No.
BUFF: Your dad's gonna wonder what happened to the car.

(Jeff doesn't answer.)

You know what we need? A hot cup of coffee. Hang on. I was up all night, too, man. Long, long night.

(Buff bops into the store and puts coffee together. Jeff approaches the pay phone and dials.)

JEFF: Yes, uh, I'd like to report . . . excuse me? Yeah. Hello? Yes, I'd like to report a . . . a . . . crime. Why do I have to tell you my name? No, it's not "in progress," it happened already. Well, no I didn't see it exactly. No. I had nothing do with it! Yeah. OK. I'll wait. *(Hangs up)*

(Buff returns and sits on the bench.)

BUFF: Calling Sooze?
JEFF: No.
BUFF: She stayed at the Four Seasons last night. But you shouldn't worry about that.
JEFF: I'm not.
BUFF: Life is too short, you know?
JEFF: I'm *not*. Worrying.
BUFF: Good.

(Jeff finds a seat next to Buff.)

JEFF: Buff, if I tell you something, would you promise not to tell anyone?
BUFF: Sure.
JEFF: I mean—no one.

BUFF: Hey, you know me.

JEFF: This is serious.

BUFF: Yeah?

JEFF: Last night . . .

BUFF: I should have stuck up for you, man, I know. You're my friend, she's your old lady. I feel bad about that. But I was *busy*, you know?

JEFF: No, this isn't about Sooze . . . She stayed at the hotel with Pony, huh?

BUFF: We *all* stayed at the hotel, man. I hung out with Danny, Pony's manager? Really nice guy. Danny says maybe I can come along for the rest of the tour and shoot all the back-stage shit, you know? They don't need a professional for that.

JEFF: Buff, listen to me for a second . . .

BUFF: I know what you're going to say. I don't know shit about making a video. But that's a *plus*, because since I'm just starting out, I have a raw look. Which is good, you know, for marketing and demographics . . .

JEFF: Buff . . .

BUFF: But, hey, I'd do it for free, you know, just for my reel.

JEFF: Yeah. OK. But listen to me—

BUFF: And guess who showed up?

JEFF: No. *Wait a second!* I have to tell you this. Tim . . .

BUFF: Yeah, Tim?

JEFF: No, Tim . . . Tim is in trouble . . .

BUFF: I know, man.

JEFF: You know?

BUFF: That's what I'm trying to tell you. That chick Erica . . .

JEFF: She's still missing, isn't she?

BUFF: Missing? No, man! She showed up at the hotel! And we had this great time together. I stayed in her room last night. What can I say?

JEFF: You saw Erica last night?

BUFF: I saw *all* of Erica last night.

JEFF: Buff, stop making shit up. It didn't happen.

BUFF: Sure it did.

JEFF: Erica . . . Listen, Tim beat the shit out of her. *(Pulling Erica's Blackberry from his pocket)* Yeah, I mean, look, I found this on the path back there. It's her Blackberry thing. She wouldn't leave it behind. And I think I saw blood on the floor of the van.

BUFF *(Taking the Blackberry from Jeff)*: Tim? When?

JEFF: Last night! He took her back to the van and . . .

(Buff jumps up, agitated. He walks away.)

BUFF: Bullshit!

JEFF: He beat her up! Bad.

BUFF: Total and utter bullshit. Look!

(Erica enters. Freshly up, smiling, happy.)

ERICA: Good morning!

(Erica and Buff kiss. She pulls him close and grabs his ass. They remain in a loose embrace eyeing each other.)

Don't look at me, I'm a mess. I'm completely burnt out!

BUFF: How'd you get burnt out?

ERICA: Playing with something *very* hot.
(Noticing Jeff holding her Blackberry) Oh, my God, you found it! Thank you so much! *(Taking her Blackberry from Jeff)* Jeff, have you been here all night?

JEFF: More or less.

ERICA: Amazing. *(To Buff)* Did you get your tape?

BUFF: Yup.

ERICA: Don't you have a bag or anything?

BUFF: I have my toothbrush.

ERICA: He's so cute!

BUFF *(To Jeff)*: I have to show my video to Danny at the hotel. If
   I get the gig, Erica's gonna teach me how to surf. In L.A.
ERICA: I'll teach you to surf, even if you don't get the gig.
BUFF: I can come visit?
ERICA: I think I can find you some place to stay.

   *(Erica and Buff fall into each other and kiss. Erica gets self-
   conscious in front of Jeff.)*

   I'll wait for you in the limo.
BUFF: OK.
ERICA: It was nice meeting you, Jeff. If you're ever in Los Angeles,
   you should drop by the offices. I talked to Pony this
   morning and he told me he's really looking forward to
   reading your songs.
JEFF: Tell Pony to fuck himself.
ERICA *(Sunny)*: I'll do that.

   *(Erica turns to go. She gives Buff a hurry-up look and exits.
   Buff watches. Beat.)*

BUFF *(To Jeff)*: She looks pretty healthy to me. *(Bops back over to
   the defeated Jeff and sits next to him)* Tim never laid a finger
   on her. He just got pissed off because she wouldn't suck
   his limp alcoholic dick. She said he was crying 'cause he
   couldn't get it up. She was laughing her ass off about it,
   you know?

   (Buff spies Tim arriving with a six-pack.)

   Oh shit!

   *(Tim sits, drinks. The three friends sit in silence. Finally Buff
   stands.)*

So, dude, gotta boogie. And listen, if I never come back, I'll send you a video of me surfin'. Get some rest, man.

(Buff tries to do some kind of complex slap/snap handshake with Jeff, but Jeff is not into it. Buff exits.)

TIM: So, did I call it? She stayed the night, didn't she? Stayed at the hotel with the rock star.

JEFF: You lied to me.

TIM: No, I didn't.

JEFF: You told me you beat up that girl.

TIM: Don't blame me 'cause you're a chump.

JEFF: No. No, that isn't the way it is, at all. I stayed up all night trying to figure out how to protect my best friend. I was trying to come up with some lie so you wouldn't have to go to jail for the next ten years.

TIM: You did that? For me?

JEFF: Yes.

TIM: Then all I can say, Jeff, is you're a fool *and* a chump.

JEFF: Why? Because I give a shit? Because I care about you?

TIM: You care about me? Touching.

(Jeff jumps up.)

JEFF: No. No. *Fuck that!* You lied to me. You lied to me because you're gutless. You're a gutless, drunken loser.

TIM: I'm a drunk. And I'm a loser. But I'm not gutless. *(He drinks)*

JEFF: It's ten o'clock in the morning. What are you drinking for?

TIM: She took me into that van. Spoiled little princess took me into the van, and she laughed at me. I'm tired of being laughed at. The pilots, the people with money, these greaseballs. Let me ask you something, Jeff, you saw that brown bitch in there point her gun at me yesterday. You think she was going to use it?

JEFF: She didn't point it at you. She was scared.

TIM: You think after we left, her and Muhammad had a nice laugh?

JEFF: No!

TIM: Well, I disagree. I think they did. I think he probably went out with his friends later and had a good laugh about the drunken vet. Makes me sick.

(Tim reaches under his sweatshirt and pulls out a Colt .45.)

JEFF: Go home. Stop drinking. Go home and sleep it off.

TIM: Sleep what off? What should I sleep off, Jeff? My life? I should go home and go to sleep, and when I wake up, what will I be? A pilot? A Super Bowl quarterback? Maybe a rock star? I don't think so.

JEFF: Just go home.

TIM: This *is* my home.

JEFF: What good does it do to start this? They never hurt you.

TIM: Sure they have. Every day! They hurt me every day, with their attitude. Putting me down! Lecturing me! Who the fuck do they think they are? I was born here.

JEFF: They're people. They have feelings.

TIM: What about my feelings? What about my FUCKING FEELINGS?

(When Tim gets loud, Pakeesa alerts Nazeer. Nazeer emerges from the store.)

I HAD A LIFE! THEY TOOK IT FROM ME! THEY COME OVER HERE AND THEY KNOW ALL THE ANSWERS! AND THEY KNOW SHIT! WELL, I'M THE NEW TEACHER!

(Nazeer sees Tim's .45.)

NAZEER: What is this now?

TIM: You call the cops, I'll come in there and blow your fucking brains out.

NAZEER: I don't have to call the cops. We don't need the cops.

TIM: Call your sister. Have her fight your fights for you.

NAZEER: I don't have to call my sister.

(Jeff moves away from Tim.)

TIM: Stay there, Jeff.

> *(To Nazeer, indicating his gun)* What are you going to do about this?

(Nazeer reaches behind his back where he has Pakeesa's .38-special in his waistband.)

NAZEER: I think you should go.

TIM: You fucking sandnigger. Terrorist!

NAZEER: Why do you call me names? I never hurt you. I'm just working here.

TIM: That's the problem.

(Jeff steps between them.)

JEFF: Wait a minute. This is ridiculous. *(To Nazeer)* What's your name?

NAZEER: What do you care?

JEFF: Maybe if we knew names, you know, things wouldn't get like this. My name is Jeff.

(Nazeer and Tim shift their positions attempting to keep an eye on each another.)

NAZEER: Norman.

JEFF: Norman what?

NAZEER: My name is Nazeer Chaudhry. Norman is . . . just a name.

JEFF: Nazeer! What's that, Indian?

TIM: Jeff, stop!

NAZEER: Pakistani. Karachi is in Pakistan.

JEFF: You know, I wanted to ask you last night, Nazeer. You like living in America?

NAZEER: It's not a choice of whether I like it or not. I'm here.

TIM *(To Jeff)*: What's wrong with you?

JEFF: Tim . . .

(Tim climbs up to the roof.)

TIM *(To Jeff)*: You have no respect for yourself.

NAZEER: Get off my property now.

TIM: Or what? You gonna shoot me?

NAZEER: OK. It's enough. Time to go. All right.

PAKEESA *(Coming from the store; in Urdu)*: I've called the police.

NAZEER: No police, now.

PAKEESA *(In Urdu)*: Yes. Enough of this! *(In English)* You know, my brother, he's such a smart guy. He has all these plans, all these big ideas because he's so smart. But he's not so smart. Because every time he makes a plan, it turns to shit. *(To Nazeer; in Urdu)* I've had it.

NAZEER: Go inside.

TIM: Now what you gonna do?

NAZEER *(To Jeff)*: Tell him to come down.

JEFF: Tim, let's go.

TIM: Give me one good reason.

JEFF: I'm asking you.

TIM: You're a fool. I don't go anywhere with fools.

(Jeff gives up. He walks away, moving to the side of the store, to think. He ventures to the back.)

NAZEER: Get down off my property.

TIM: Fuck you!

NAZEER: I *will* call the police.

TIM: Go ahead! They love you almost as much as I do. Hey, Ma, look at me! I'm on the top of the world, Ma!

NAZEER: Get off my roof! You bum! You drunk!

(Pakeesa barks a few words at Nazeer in Urdu. Jeff moves to Tim, talking to him from below.)

PAKEESA *(In Urdu)*: Ye kya hoora hain? *(Can you take care of this now?)* Enough!

TIM *(Singing)*: Here she comes to save the day!

NAZEER: Get down, now!

TIM: Shoot me! Shoot me, right here! You know you want to!

(Beat. Nazeer seems to consider the option.)

You'd be doing me a fucking favor! Do it! Come on! Do it!

(Jeff returns from behind the store, carrying Bee-Bee's limp body.)

JEFF: Tim. Tim, get down here. *(To Nazeer)* Help me.

NAZEER: Is she drunk? Take her home!

PAKEESA *(In Urdu)*: What's wrong with her?

TIM: Is that Bee-Bee? What's wrong with her? *(He climbs down)*

(Jeff gently lays Bee-Bee on the ground. He stays with her.)

JEFF: She's unconscious! Call 911! Bee-Bee! Bee-Bee! Wake up!

(Pakeesa runs into the store.)

TIM *(On the pay phone to 911)*: Yeah. Hi. You know the convenience store on 9? Yeah, the one just before the KFC. We need an ambulance over here. Right now. *(To Nazeer)* You're fucked now, dude. *(Into the phone)* I don't know. Just send it. OK. I'm holding.

JEFF *(Trying to rouse her)*: BEE-BEE!

TIM *(To Nazeer)*: I hope you're happy.

NAZEER: This has nothing to do with me. This . . . this drinking.

TIM: It has *everything* to do with you. My friend. *(Into the phone)* Yes I'm still holding.

NAZEER: No, she went back there . . .

TIM: It's *your* property, it's *your* problem.

JEFF: Tim, something's really wrong with her!

(Sirens are heard in the distance.)

NAZEER: My sister called the police. They are coming.

TIM: Fuck. *(Hangs up the pay phone angrily)*

PAKEESA *(Coming back outside; in Urdu, pointing at Bee-Bee)*: Ye log bilgul pagal hogain. Theiko, theiko! *(In English)* These people are completely insane! Look! Look! *(As if to say, "I told you so!" to her brother)*

JEFF: They coming?

(Tim steps toward Nazeer, ignoring Jeff.)

TIM: You're going to be so sorry you ever showed your brown face in this town.

JEFF: She doesn't have any pulse, Tim! She's cold!

PAKEESA *(To Nazeer)*: What's wrong with her?

NAZEER: I don't know! I don't know! Go in the store! *(She does. To Jeff)* What is wrong with her?

TIM: She's dead.

JEFF: No, she isn't! Tim! We have to . . . How do you do this?

(Jeff pushes on Bee-Bee's chest. He leans over to give her mouth-to-mouth, pulling her head back, trying to figure it out. Tim reaches down and pulls him back by the shoulder.)

TIM: Jeff! Stop! She's gone. She's cold. OK!

JEFF *(In shock; turning to Tim)*: What?

TIM: When they get here they'll know what to do.

NAZEER: This has nothing to do with me, you know. She went back there by herself. I tell you over and over, don't drink on my property. Don't drink on my property. He's bull-shitting, right? How can she be dead?

JEFF: She's . . . she's not . . .

(Jeff crumples over Bee-Bee and begins to cry.
Tim calmly sits and waits, watching Jeff and Bee-Bee.)

NAZEER: She's not dead. They will come and take care of her. I'm going inside. I can't look at this. *(As he heads into the store)* YOU PEOPLE ARE SO STUPID!

(Nazeer comes back out of the store. He speaks with quiet deliberation, speaking to Tim, Jeff, even Bee-Bee:)

What is wrong with you?! Can you tell me? What?! What?! You don't know! Throw it all away! You throw it all away! What do you think is going to happen, what do you think? Oh God. Oh God. This is hell.

(Nazeer slowly walks back into the store. The sirens get louder and louder. They are almost upon us.
Jeff straightens up, picks up Bee-Bee's limp hand, and holds it, gently.
Tim watches him.
Lights down.)

END OF PLAY

Eric Bogosian wrote and starred in the play *Talk Radio* (The Public Theater, 1987). It was revived in 2007 for Broadway and starred Liev Schreiber. For this work he was nominated for a Pulitzer Prize and a Tony Award. For his film adaptation of *Talk Radio*, Bogosian received the Berlin Film Festival "Silver Bear." His six solo performances Off-Broadway between 1980 and 2000 (including *Drinking in America*; *Sex, Drugs, Rock & Roll* and *Wake Up and Smell the Coffee*) received three OBIE awards. In addition to *Talk Radio*, Bogosian has written a number of full-length plays, including *subUrbia* (Lincoln Center Theater, Second Stage Theatre, also adapted as a film), *Griller* (The Goodman Theatre), *Red Angel* (Williamstown Theatre Festival), *Humpty Dumpty* (McCarter Theatre Center) and *1+1* (New York Stage and Film). He is the author of three novels: *Mall*, *Wasted Beauty* and *Perforated Heart* and a novella *Notes from Underground*. As an actor, Bogosian has appeared in numerous films and television programs, including Robert Altman's *The Caine Mutiny Court Martial*; Oliver Stone's *Talk Radio*; *Under Siege II*; *Wonderland*; and as a continuing character on *Law & Order: Criminal Intent*. Visit: www.ericbogosian.com